GOODBYE, BRITAIN?

TONY ALDOUS

SIDGWICK & JACKSON LONDON

To Vivian

Previous pages: Urban
motorways often form
barriers to people on
foot, severing
neighbourhoods and
disrupting
communities.
Pedestrian routes
provided as
substitutes tend to be,
like this one under
the north side of
Glasgow's motorway
box, hostile and
wearyingly off-
putting to the
pedestrian

First published in
Great Britain in 1975
by Sidgwick and
Jackson Limited
Copyright © 1975 by
Tony Aldous
Foreword copyright
© 1975 by Sir John
Betjeman

ISBN 0 283 98102 4

Design by Paul Watkins
Picture research by
Anne-Marie Ehrlich

Filmset by Keyspools
Limited, Golborne,
Lancashire
Printed and bound in Great Britain by
REDWOOD BURN Limited
Trowbridge and Esher

for Sidgwick and
Jackson Limited
1 Tavistock Chambers,
Bloomsbury Way
London WC1A 2SG

GOODBYE, BRITAIN?

CONTENTS

FOREWORD by Sir John Betjeman

The strength of this book is its restraint. Tony Aldous, when he was Environmental Correspondent to *The Times,* showed his gift for writing readably, clearly and shortly about complicated planning matters. It is good that he has carried his talent out into a full-length book with effective illustrations.

The tradition of topographical writing in Great Britain is long and strong. In the eighteenth century it was manifested in engraved topographical works and later in books on the picturesque with aquatints of lakes, mountains, clumps of trees and ruins. These books were an interpretation of English scenery in terms of Claude Lorraine and Nicholas Poussin.

In the first quarter of the nineteenth century when Birmingham and Liverpool were booming, topographical writers envisaged a perfect England in the Middle Ages with benevolent abbots, hopeful pilgrims and the mutter of the mass faintly heard through gilded screens. Pugin was inspired by his dreams of a perfect 1440 to caricature the Greek revival of 1840 and the Strawberry Hill gothic which preceded it.

Ruskin and Morris in the latter half of the nineteenth century idealized the worker craftsman. Hand-made was thought better than machine-made. At the beginning of this century topographical writers had in mind a perfect society of villagers. Country was healthier, and a more natural way of living than in a town. The Cotswolds were preferable to the sunny stucco terraces of Brighton. After the Second World War the Georgian style became the ideal of topographers. The desecration of country with hoardings and petrol-stations and poles and wires (pylons had not yet got into their stride) was inveighed against by such pioneers as Sir Clough Williams-Ellis and Sir Herbert Read, the Council for the Protection of Rural England, the Society for the Protection of Ancient Buildings and the National Trust. Numerous Ramblers' Associations tried to protect villages and 'countryside' (as it is always called by those who are not farmers) from jerry-built villas and urbanization.

After the Second World War the word 'develop' was beginning to mean 'destroy'. 'Comprehensive development' was jargon for 'total destruction'. The Americanization of English and making six words take the place of one, the soft lies of public relations officers, were lulling us into acceptance of 'housing' instead of houses. The house itself became a 'machine to live in'. Language became hysterical as mine is becoming as I write this at the thought of England becoming a few acres of preserved countryside between concrete fly-overs, spanned by cafeterias thrumming with canned music and reeking of grease.

It was generally thought twenty years ago that only old fogies looking back to a never-never land of William Morris and garden cities objected to dehumanizing skyscraper blocks of flats and what Tony Aldous rightly calls 'highwaymen' meaning road engineers. Tony Aldous has no illusions.

Since the last war the destruction of our towns, especially the less important and less obviously historic of them, has gone on faster even than the destruction of the country. Not even the Civic Trust, founded with remarkable foresight by Lord Duncan Sandys, has stayed the developer who would sooner demolish than restore. This book shows in photographs the havoc created in tourist-free and therefore natural towns like Tamworth and Northampton, the terrible destruction in Newcastle, Bristol and the City of London. But Tony Aldous explains how it came about. His is an encouraging book for it also shows how we can best preserve what is left of our background and our birthright, the houses, lanes, trees, shops, inns, church-towers and railway-stations which may not be great architecture or masterpieces to art historians but which still represent what we mean by home. The developer's chief ally is generally the medical officer of health, his innocent victim. Usually he works through the local council. But legislation, as Lord Kennet showed in his book *Preservation* (1972), is catching up with the developer. In the Department of the Environment we have a court of appeal against threats to our eyes and ears and noses by builders, engineers and manufacturers. We must go about it calmly by protesting through all the legal channels, first a letter to the local paper – journalists are the allies of our environment because they are trained to use their eyes and to sense public feeling. Next write to the local protection society which may or may not be allied with the Civic Trust. In the last resort write to the Department of the Environment, if necessary at its headquarters in London. The motto there is 'Patch and mend. Don't demolish. Make the best of what is there already.'

INTRODUCTION

THE physical fabric of Britain – how it looks, feels, and even sounds – has changed dramatically in the two decades 1954–74. This change has probably been greater overall than all the changes of the preceding twenty centuries. Yet we have become so accustomed, even if not inured, to the present scale and pace of change that we are in danger of losing sight of what is involved.

Let me give an example. A man visiting his dentist in Baker Street recently after a year's absence could not find the building. He hunted from end to end of the street. It was just not where it used to be. Finally, checking against the very few premises that now display street numbers, he tracked it down. It was not so much that the door had been painted a different colour, or that the coffee shop at the corner had become a Greek restaurant with a different kind of shopfront. That block relatively speaking was the same as when he had first gone there fifteen years previously. But almost everything else in that part of the street had changed. The Georgian terraces had one by one been surrounded by demolition men's hoardings. Block by block they had fallen, to be replaced by taller, no doubt more efficient, but totally un-memorable office blocks. It unhinged that dentist's patient's normally acute sense of direction. He was struck down by an affliction peculiarly common in our times: to be lost in your own town.

In the countryside, as we shall see in chapters 9 and 10, the changes may be every bit as drastic as these. Technology and chemistry have vastly increased man's power to alter, in the cause of efficiency or economics, the whole shape and texture of the landscape. And there, increasingly, as in the towns, a public that was first impressed by the changes, then bewildered by them, has become steadily more disenchanted with them. The reaction has often reached the point where public opinion as a whole distrusts almost any change – or, at least, almost any change affecting that part of its environment with which it is in daily or frequent contact. So strong is this reaction that, in the last year or two, increasing mutterings of concern have come from many members of those professions whose job it is to guide, and design for, change (notably architects and civil engineers) to the effect that 'the preservation pendulum has swung too far'. What this generally means is (a) that they cannot as easily get their schemes accepted without entanglement in public controversy; and (b) that public distrust of all change obstructs the beneficial and necessary, the sensitively and attractively designed building or structure as well as the brash, destructive and brutal.

Disapproval of blanket resistance to change is, however, rarely accompanied by any serious examination of the causes of such attitudes. Contrary to what is often assumed, aesthetics are only the tip of a very much larger iceberg. Other factors are social and psychological. Reaction against rule by technology and accountancy may be another ingredient. The question which once loomed largest in people's minds, 'Can we do it?', is now increasingly replaced by another, 'Should we do it?' Thus, for example, aesthetic reaction is not the main ingredient in the bad odour surrounding the Centre Point office tower at Tottenham Court Road in London. Given the dictates of the client's brief, plot ratio and site, Seifert's tall tower in precast concrete units is not a bad solution from a visual architectural point of view. But aesthetic judgements have been clouded by strong feelings about the social implications: money and resources poured into a building which for a decade has remained empty while, for lack of such money and resources, people remained homeless; and the fact that the building's owner, Harry Hyams, achieved huge capital gains from a building which, during that period, was a huge social and financial minus to the community. Unlike the modest buildings it replaced, Centre Point provided neither jobs nor commercial custom for the area surrounding it.

Social losses accrue from public as well as private development, however. Much of the opposition to urban motorways, for instance, stems not just from destruction of people's homes and the inadequacy of the compensation or rehousing offered. It is rooted in fear of change, dislocation of the community, and disruption of people's lives and patterns of movement. Research undertaken for the government's Urban Motorways Committee[1] showed, to most people's surprise, that 'severance' was a bigger factor than traffic noise in people's worries about nearby major road building.

These fears are extensive, widespread, and no great respecters of class or status. They suggest one of the key differences between the attitudes of people in the sixties and seventies to environmental change and those of previous decades. It is the scale of it all that frightens. Five yards of your garden taken for a modest road widening in the 1950s was one thing; the transformation of your whole surroundings by a 100ft wide swathe of concrete and asphalt and relentless alien movement is quite another. The scale of change in many people's minds has become inhuman. Instead of the quiet though perhaps tatty little footpath or lane between gardens which granny used to follow to the shops, she now finds the civil engineers expect her to use a subway that is little better than a dark and smelly drain. Instead

of a street with frequent doors and windows and evidence of people, the architect gives us a blank podium 100 yards long, broken only by one well-finished but windowless teak fire exit.

Rapidity as well as scale of change also confuses and frightens people. Ashley Barker, the G.L.C.'s Surveyor of Historic Buildings, has made the point that one important quality people desire in the places they inhabit is a continuing and recognizable identity. He sees the public mood as having changed in the last century and a half. 'Until Queen Victoria's reign even city life had been lived, for the most part, among surroundings which changed slowly enough to make novelty and redevelopment agreeable aspects of existence, to be welcomed wholeheartedly as a spice of life. In such conditions, the occasional disappearance of the old-fashioned and outmoded to make way for a later and "improved" taste could be approved by most people. There would no doubt be times when private grief might have been felt at the loss of a building or a vista which held special memories or gave particular pleasure to an individual; but, if I am right in thinking that when we consider the surroundings required for contentment, a delicate balance must exist between the past, the present and the promised future, then only a dedicated antiquary would have felt the need to arrest change in those days.'[2]

That phrase 'the surroundings required for contentment' is, I think, a significant one. Though life in the 1970s has a fair amount of surprise and variety, we are short on contentment. Fewer and fewer new buildings and structures have looked comfortable and at home with their neighbours. We have now, says Ashley Barker, 'reached the point where, sadly as it may seem, many people are opposed to any new development, so keenly do they feel the need for stability and so disenchanted are they with the new worlds they see rising.'[3] He makes it plain that he is talking here, not of architectural niceties appreciated only by the connoisseur, but about the rest of us, the untutored laymen who care. 'The man on the Clapham omnibus and the man from Philadelphia feel the need as never before to see in the city the evidence of its past.'[4] This book is written for them. 'A town without a past is like a man without a memory,'[5] some perceptive old conservationist once remarked. In the last few years Britain has teetered on the brink of rampant, self-inflicted, chronic amnesia. There are signs that we are now stepping back. It will be none too soon. We need pause to absorb and recover.

Acknowledgements of help and sources is always difficult. A journalist builds with so much material from different sources, and even in attempting to thank for help given specifically with this book in mind, I may unintentionally miss some whose aid I would wish to acknowledge. They include: Lewis Braithwaite who showed me much in Tamworth and Birmingham; Pamela Lock and the Bath Preservation Trust; Peter Willis and Brian Jobling in Newcastle; Chris Curtis and Patrick Brown in Bristol; Colin Robinson in Northampton; Chris Hall; the Youth Hostels Association; Theo Burrell and Reg Hookway on the countryside; Christopher Hanson-Smith and Geoffrey Berry in the Lakes; Lawrence Rich at Petworth and for coastline data; Dr William Stanton on quarrying in Mendip; Dr Robin Best for data on urbanization; Dr Peter Ambrose for the inspiration of, and permission to quote, his book *The Quiet Revolution*; George Moore, Gordon Borthwick, Colin McWilliam, Alan Thompson, Peter Allan and Adrian Varwell in Scotland; Tony and Elizabeth Roberts in Pembrokeshire; and John Earl for his invaluable advice, knowledge and inspiration in the London chapters. I also wish to thank Jenny Spallone for bearing the main burden of retyping my pockmarked and potholed draft typescript; William Armstrong of Sidgwick and Jackson for persuading me to write the book and so patiently awaiting its arrival; Jan Widdows and Paul Watkins for turning mere text into actual bound book; and to Sir Nikolaus Pevsner, to whose *Buildings of England* series more than any other work I most constantly refer. And finally to Vivian, Simon, Kate and Jessica for their remarkable patience and good humour in the protracted and taxing period of production.

TONY ALDOUS
Blackheath
August 1974

1. *Report of the Urban Motorways Project Team*, H.M.S.O., 1973
2. Barker, Ashley, *Chartered Surveyor*, September 1972, p. 117
3. Barker, op. cit., p. 118
4. Barker, op. cit., p. 119
5. Quoted in the Civic Trust's award-winning film, *A Future for Our Past*

1 THE DESTRUCTION O
THE REASONS WHY

BRITISH towns in the past two or three decades have been subject to two main types of pressure for physical change: redevelopment of their buildings – most often for new housing or to provide larger and more modern shopping and commercial areas – and the building of bigger and bigger new roads to cope with the ever-increasing volumes of traffic generated in an age of mass motor-car ownership. These are, as John Harvey puts it in his *Conservation of Buildings*, the 'two main enemies, acting in unholy alliance against all the traditional values of the urban and rural scene'.[1] And indeed they are closely connected. Town centre redevelopment, for instance, tends to generate very large increases in motor vehicle use. Conversely, new roads coming into or close to a town bring about powerful pressures for physical change in the urban fabric itself. Nonetheless, for convenience's sake, we deal with roads and traffic mostly in Chapter 12, The Highwaymen. This present chapter is devoted to the impact of demolition and replacement of buildings on the character and life of towns – though the two themes are inseparable and this demarcation line is sometimes crossed.

At first sight it might appear that two quite different kinds of town have been affected by redevelopment, with two different sets of considerations applying: historic and beautiful towns such as Bath, York, Oxford or Winchester, where any development arguably harms a delicate picture unless it is minimal in scale and skilfully sympathetic in manner; and towns, or areas of towns, where considerable 'renewal' is unquestionably needed, and the argument turns on the nature of the redevelopment to be adopted. The Council for British Archaeology's oft-quoted shorter list[2] of fifty-one historic towns 'so splendid and precious' that their care ought to be a national responsibility, might be taken as a rough guide to our first category. In the other group one might expect to see towns like Birmingham, Coventry, Newcastle and Glasgow.

The more we look at it, however, the less tenable this distinction proves. In the first place, beauty and history have not stopped the people and local authorities in undoubtedly fine old towns from wanting the jobs and prosperity which it seemed to them only redevelopment could bring. Secondly, the issue was confused until very recently by the tendency (which still to some extent exists) to think of a historic town not as an overall whole, a community part of whose heritage is a familiar and attractive townscape, but as a series of set-pieces, individual historic buildings more or less independent of their surroundings. I have cited this distinction elsewhere[3] as one of the key differences between preservation and conservation.* Belated appreciation

* This discussion of the meanings of the word 'conservation' and the ways in which it differs from 'preservation' is reproduced on p. 190

that the whole was something more than the sum of individual parts was greatly advanced by the Civic Trust's pioneering of the 1967 Civic Amenities Act with its concept of the conservation area; but by then much of the damage had been done or redevelopment based on the 'historic building in aspic' approach was so far committed as to be irreversible.

Before we look at some examples of bad (and good) redevelopment in historic towns, however, let us consider the other side of the coin: large, mainly nineteenth- and twentieth-century cities where it might be thought there was nothing worth keeping. In Birmingham and Glasgow, Newcastle and Northampton, the ignorant stranger might suppose there was little or nothing worth preserving. Indeed, in the face of urgent and authoritative testimony to the contrary, some city fathers of Glasgow were in the year of environmental enlightenment, 1972, still asserting this.[4]

1. Harvey, John, *Conservation of Buildings*, John Baker, 1972, p. 40
2. Council for British Archaeology: Memorandum *Historic Towns*, July 1965. See also *The Erosion of History*, Council for British Archaeology, 1972. The towns are: Abingdon, Cambridge, Wisbech, Cockermouth, Whitehaven, Totnes, Blandford, Barnard Castle, Colchester, Thaxted, Chipping Campden, Tewkesbury, Hereford, Sandwich, Lincoln, Stamford, King's Lynn, Norwich, Wymondham, Newcastle on Tyne, Newark on Trent, Burford, Oxford, Bridgnorth, Ludlow, Bath, Wells, Hadleigh, Lavenham, Lewes, Rye, Warwick, Bradford on Avon, Marlborough, Salisbury, Pershore, Beverley, Richmond, Scarborough, York, Conway, Monmouth, Tenby, Aberdeen, Inveraray, Haddington, Culross, Edinburgh and Leith, Cromarty, Kelso, Stirling.
3. *Outlook*, Bristol & West Building Society, winter 1971
4. Councillor Tom Fulton, convener of the Highways Committee, told a meeting of Glasgow City Council in November 1971 that 'the director of planning had said that the East Flank [motorway] line created no difficulty for them. Apart from the Tollbooth, there were no buildings in the High Street worth retaining. It was a damned scandal that conservationists talked about areas of the city about which they knew nothing'. (*Glasgow Herald* 12 November 1971) Buildings in the High Street included Charles Rennie Mackintosh's Martyrs' School (whose proposed demolition drew a rare protest from the Royal Institute of British Architects – see page 167) and the 18th century College Residences by James and Robert Adam. The effect of the road on buildings it missed also promised to be environmentally ruinous.

ONE city where, arguably, the greater part of the built-up area and its adjacent open spaces should have been put, visually speaking, in aspic, is Bath. The whole of the pre-twentieth-century city might justifiably have been made, not so much a conservation area as a 'preservation area'. For the beauty of Bath is more than the sum of its major architectural glories. It consists also in two rare and outstanding qualities: the relationship between Georgian architecture and surrounding landscape; and the completeness of the Georgian townscape, with orderly terrace after orderly terrace climbing and running along the contours of the bowl of hills that contains the Georgian town.

In theory there was never any dispute that 'Bath ought to be preserved'. The dispute – and there has been plenty of it in the past two decades – turned on the nature and extent of the Bath that merited preservation, and the degree and nature or replacement and renewal that were necessary and permissible. The great set-pieces of Royal Crescent and the Circus, at the one end of the scale, were scarcely in doubt, though money for the restoration was by no means readily forthcoming in the 1950s.

Previous pages: One of Bath's great architectural set-pieces, Royal Crescent; and (inset) Birmingham's Bull Ring Centre covered shopping precinct

Below: Bath's new Beaufort Hotel wrecks a familiar and cherished view of Pulteney Bridge. Right: The car park podium for the proposed law courts is totally unsympathetic to the Georgian city about it

These were listed Grade 1 buildings, the most glittering jewels in the diadem. But, as Adam Fergusson has shown in his passionate and in some ways bitter account of the post-war fate of the city, *The Sack of Bath*,[1] the city council in aiding and abetting redevelopment (other people's and its own) was no great respecter of Grade 2 buildings and quite ruthless in its treatment of the statutorily unprotected Grade 3s (now the 'local list') 'which would certainly have been considered for statutorily protection in almost any other town'.

During the thirteen years from 1950 to 1973, more than 1,000 Georgian buildings were demolished in Bath. They included well over 350 officially 'listed' buildings, some whose listing was only advisory but many with statutory protection. In 1968 the city council was only just prevented from wrecking the precincts of Bath Abbey by demolishing a key early nineteenth-century building, Kingston Buildings (which now houses the planning department), and erecting in its place a 'sensible' new office block. Unhappily they could not be deterred from clearing (with central government approval or at least acquiescence) an area north of Pulteney Bridge on which was built, despite angry

public protest, an out-of-character and out-of-scale new hotel. Its height and bulk, as well as the ugly extract tower from the garage below, ruin for ever the vista of Pulteney Bridge from down river.

Alongside the hotel the city council itself constructed the very ugly podium for a new law courts building, plans for which had at the time of writing been submitted to the Royal Fine Art Commission but not publicly displayed.[2] It is, however, difficult to imagine that even the most skilful design could accommodate in the centre of Bath the spaces needed for a modern courts building and its ancillary offices and cells, without further seriously damaging the scale and character of the riverside and the heart of the city. As to the podium, this kind of structure – a six-foot-high blank wall running a hundred feet or more – is entirely alien to a Georgian street, whose walls are, or should be, at ground level an orderly but varied procession of doors and windows, columns, railings and porticos. Whether such a blank wall is clad in brown or grey aggregate panels or in reconstituted Bath stone or even in real ashlar, it is almost bound to be an alien presence. Certainly this one does irredeemable damage. Irredeemable, that is, short of its demolition.

How can this attitude on the part of the citizens and city fathers of England's finest Georgian city be explained? We can, I think, pinpoint six major reasons:

(1) First, quite simply profit motive, seen by some preservationists rather too simplistically as 'the greed which wantonly destroys our heritage'. It is, however, not necessarily immoral to want to replace an inefficient old building with a more efficient and profitable new one; nor even for a local council to hanker after the extra rate revenue that such a change promises. And in the late 1950s and early sixties that was the prevailing climate, in Bath as elsewhere. What can be said is that in Bath, where the size and completeness of the architectural heritage should have ensured a certain circumspection and tenderness in the wielding of the knife, the city cut away with the ruthlessness of a man who never questions that the 'dead wood' must go if the tree is to survive. Some people found it significant that, at least until local government reorganization, what would in most towns have been the planning committee still, in Bath, proudly called itself the Development Committee. Whatever the law might say about presumption in favour of retention of Grade 2 buildings, in any conflict between that and substantial development the onus was, in reality, on the preservationists to overturn what may be dubbed 'the rule of justifiable redevelopment'.

(2) Intertwined with this, and more powerful in social and planning terms, ran the argument that, just because a town had a fine architectural heritage, that did not mean it should or could stand still. 'Develop or decline' was the municipal watchword. Historic towns could not live by history alone, but needed jobs and prosperity if they were not to languish and (so the argument ran) even the finest buildings risk decay. So you allowed the developer, public or private, to demolish and rebuild, requiring him to 'respect the character' of the town in the design of his new buildings. You also sanctioned new roads, for without them you feared the new development would be strangled.

You did all this, as we have seen, ostensibly to protect the great set-pieces for whose restoration money was now being painfully and slowly found. You did so because (3) 'everyone knew' that Royal Crescent and The Circus, Gay Street and Broad Street, Brock Street and Milsom Street, Pulteney Bridge and Queen Square, were the glory of Georgian Bath, the bits that really mattered. If these could be saved, and the place kept economically healthy, the loss of lesser terraces – often built for artisans and of no great intrinsic architectural merit – was not too much to be deplored. That was the prevailing view in the council, and those who objected risked being called cranks or sentimentalists.

(4) This in turn links with a further point of justification: the 'art of the possible' argument. Bath's city fathers and their architectural advisers were obsessed with the danger of attempting too much, of spreading the meagre funds available for restoration too thinly. And, given the relatively tiny sums offered during the fifties and sixties by central government towards the propping up and restoration of even listed historic buildings judged to be 'outstanding', they felt that they, too, had to be extremely selective. As for the rest, if you could not restore and maintain them, what was the point of striving to exclude them from development? As long as the replacements were decent and reasonably in character, what more could be expected?

A further reason (5) concerns, I suspect, the tightness of nineteenth-century municipal boundaries (even with later amendments) and the independent status as a planning authority of that now obsolete Victorian creation, the county borough. Had Bath been municipally as well as geographically part of Somerset, the outcome might have been otherwise: development might have been channelled elsewhere and the Georgian city left to crumble until conscience or a more forthcoming attitude on the part of national opinion or central government rescued it. I feel the more confident in suggesting this because, in not wholly dissimilar circumstances, the university city of Cambridge has been saved from some of the worst excesses of development.[3] And there the county for two decades prevented the town from ruining itself. Cambridgeshire, unlike Somerset, was the planning authority. But to expect the same of the planning committee of a planning authority elected only by the citizens of Bath and concerned with and confined within boundaries that run at most 1½ miles from the town centre, is another matter. Prosperity seemed to Tory businessmen and Labour trades unionists alike to mean redevelopment. And redevelopment on a new site well away from the existing centre, to take the pressure off the historic core, though a classic solution frequently adopted elsewhere, was scarcely compatible with those boundaries, let alone vested property interests. A final reason (6) recurs in discussing towns whose character has been wrecked or impoverished by redevelopment. It is that people 'did not realize' the scale or impact of the changes proposed. And 'people' includes those who might have been expected to be able to judge correctly. Bath Preservation Trust is a case in point. The Trust, a well-established and influential body in the city, for some years supported the city council's plan (adapted from proposals by Colin Buchanan and Partners) for a large-scale road through the centre of the city, carried in tunnel for about half a mile under the most sensitive 'Heritage' area.

A public campaign mounted by a formidable ginger group, the Bath Environment Campaign, infiltration of the Trust's membership by the Campaigners, and the advent of new trustees, led to a change in the management and character of the Trust. In 1971 it put its policies on the road scheme into reverse. It is significant that members of this high-powered and influential body had not previously appreciated the extent of the demolitions required nor the full visual impact of the proposed road works. This was especially true of the tunnel terminals.

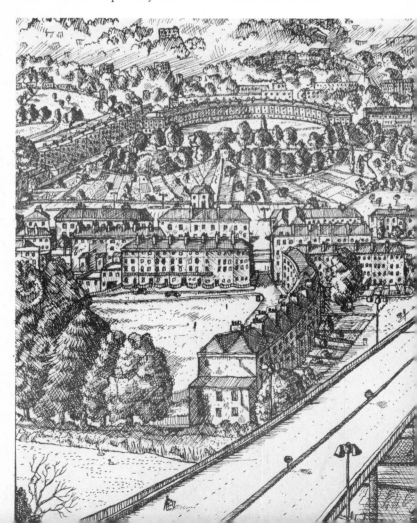

The same state of belated perception applies to the large area cleared – of what one city official called 'Georgian rubbish' – between Bath station and the line of the walls of the old medieval borough. The demolitions made way for the new Southgate Street shopping development. Most citizens did not understand or visualize the scale of demolition or of the redevelopment until the buildings had come down.[4] It certainly applies to the Walcot Street hotel/podium/law courts complex already discussed. People did not realize how much would be demolished; how large and alien the replacement would be; how close and damaging to the places and views they loved, like Pulteney Bridge; or how big an impact it would have on the overall townscape as seen from more distant viewpoints. When they did understand, demolition had already occurred; permissions been given which (even supposing an official change of heart) were too expensive to revoke. In Bath, as elsewhere, the truth dawned too late.

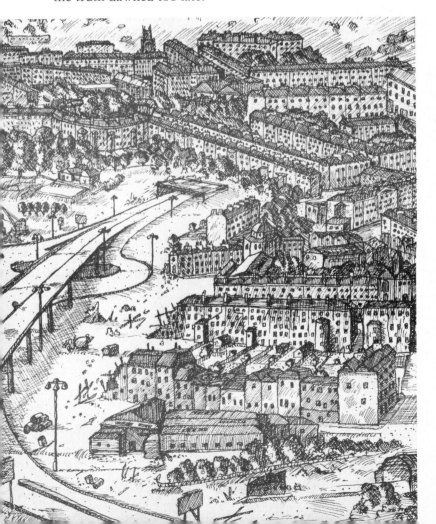

The redevelopment of Birmingham's Bull Ring area created what was, for Britain, a new kind of city centre, with impressively engineered roads running under and through buildings, purpose-built pedestrian shopping precincts, and an architecture to match its Brummie brashness

BIRMINGHAM is perhaps the classic case of a large industrial city seeking to renew its heart by redevelopment on the widespread public assumption that there was little there worth keeping. The city's strategy for renewal has been essentially an engineer's strategy, first functional and only incidentally as an afterthought concerned with aesthetics or social fabric. Its goals were to build Birmingham a vast, new shopping centre, traffic-free and under cover; to house in new buildings a greatly increased demand for office space; and in rebuilding the city centre to make on a scale never before attempted in Britain, purpose-built provision for the motor-car – on which Birmingham's prosperity hinged and to which its

citizens are devoted. It was a daringly ambitious exercise in civic engineering carrying forward dreams originally dreamed by the city's inter-war engineer, Sir Herbert Manzoni: running near-motorway standard roads to and tightly round the rebuilt centre; through and under buildings rather than simply past them; ingeniously, and expensively, stitched into the very fabric of the city. By an engineer's standards it is not only a *tour de force*, but a success: functionally it works.[6] And though they were by no means inhumane men, for most of the staff in the department of the City Engineer of the 1960s, that was the test. The omelette was judged worth its colossal breaking of eggs.

Is it? Ian Nairn, returning to look at the Bull Ring Centre's pedestrianized, covered shopping and part completed Ringway

'The city engineer's staff did their best to humanize pedestrian places cut off from their surroundings. But even with statuary, seats, tubs of plants and patches of grass, the centre of a roundabout is not a comfortable nor an attractive place to linger

system in 1967, found the changes on the whole exhilarating and in character. Thriving on affluence, the city now showed a spirit 'equal to that of a century ago, in Joe Chamberlain's heyday'.[5] Though its external architecture might be uninspiring, inside the Bull Ring Centre was 'an Aladdin's cave, a marvellous bit of interlocking design that takes a low-level bus station, a market hall and a ring-road in its stride'.[6]

By contrast, other commentators with a feel for the quality of urban environment have found the rebuilt centre's architecture abysmal, its pedestrian underpasses squalid, the Bull Ring shopping malls and those of the later New Street Centre depressing and banal. For myself, I cannot get too upset about this aspect of the new Birmingham. This is what Birmingham wanted. Bull Ring and New Street Centre together provide 574,000 sq.ft of traffic-free, weather-protected shopping. Its preponderance of repetitious tawdry multiples may not be what you or I mostly require, but it fulfils a need. It is brash and Brummie and tasteless, like one mock medieval pub interior I once visited in a new Birmingham suburb where a plastic Excalibur stood firmly embedded in its plastic stone in the place of honour alongside the juke-box. But the sandwiches and beer in that pub were good value, within their limits. So, too, within its limits, are those shopping malls. As to the quality of shopping, there is scope for improvement. The latest sections of New Street, for instance, contain an art gallery and a passable imitation of an open air 'Continental' café.

There are, however, other aspects of the redevelopment of central Birmingham that are more worrying. Sir Colin Buchanan put his finger on one of them when the AA's *Drive*[7] magazine took him to the central area in May 1971 and interviewed him with a stretch of the inner ringway as backcloth. And this dedicated promoter of the idea of new, purpose-built roads as a means to the defence and improvement of the urban environment confessed himself deeply disappointed by what he saw there. After all that expenditure and turmoil, the pedestrian was still left exposed to considerable volumes of traffic in the central core of the town, he said. In a sense, of course, the enclosed Bull Ring and New Street precincts are the bonus for the pedestrian. Yet one of the weaknesses of the Birmingham situation undoubtedly is that the city had, when Sir Colin made that visit, managed to pedestrianize only a tiny length of pre-existing shopping street.[8] Contrast this with the scope and success of the Leeds 'Paved Zone' discussed in Chapter 13.

Another feature of the rebuilt central Birmingham, often praised but in my view depressing, is the nature of the pedestrian paths and spaces alongside, within and under the new road system. Neville Borg[9] and his department tried hard to humanize these. The subways are wider and more open, not the squalid drains that are found for example at some London road intersections. Within the sunken drums of some of the roundabouts, gardens have been created and murals commissioned. Though admirable in themselves, and often an ingenious and gifted response to the constraints of site, these seem to me to be making the best of an impossible brief. Who wants to sit in a garden surrounded or overshadowed by the rush and roar of heavy traffic? At Holloway Circus on the Sparkbrook Ringway the underpasses are generous and their corners splayed to get away from the drain effect and there is, admirably – here as elsewhere under the Ringways – a newspaper kiosk and distinctive decor which helps to give the place some life and identity. But the place is vandalized: paint on the walls and a bank of telephones all wrecked. The answer is neither vandal-proof materials nor withdrawal of services. We may note that vandalism occurs disproportionately in certain kinds of redevelopment. It hits places where nobody lives; where plenty of people pass and few stop; places in which no one feels a sense of personal responsibility. Jane Jacobs, who has written penetratingly about the causes or occasions of urban violence and vandalism in *The Death and Life of Great American Cities*,[10] would probably say that the failure of those subways under the Birmingham ringways is that they have no windows and no abiding life of their own. The people there are all passing through. No one cares sufficiently or has sufficient proprietorial interest in this kind of urban space to be active in its defence. But it goes further than mere supervision. The causes and nature of vandalism are all too little understood. But it cannot be coincidence that most of the places worst hit by it are anonymous, alien, hostile places. Can it be that the vandals sometimes show better judgement than the creators of the places they despoil? That they are instinctively protesting against an ugly and hostile environment? The picture should, however, be kept in perspective. Some of the inner areas of Birmingham swept away by the construction of the ring-roads and the city's huge clearance schemes were back-to-back slums of an utterly unredeemable kind. No amount of misguided sentiment can present their demolition as anything but a blessing. What has replaced them is mixed in quality. The best is very good. Almost every year the city won awards from the old Ministry of Housing (now part of the Department of the Environment) or from the Civic Trust for housing schemes which were both good-looking and good to

Birmingham's Lea Bank development close to the city centre provided a greatly improved home environment for people from the slums if replaced (inset); the turn of the conservation tide saved the nearby Lea Terrace to give variety and a sense of continuity to the neighbourhood

30

live in. For example, the city council's Metchley Grange estate, which won the Ministry's gold medal in 1967, is a skilful mixture of low- and high-rise housing in advance of its time. It uses its site well, with the 40 per cent one- and two-storey tile-hung terraces running down to a lake and many trees retained to give the estate a maturity and lushness. The former city architect, Alan Maudsley, has been discredited by his conviction and jailing for corruption. This, however, does not detract from the high quality of many schemes which the department's architects and landscape architects achieved under him. Even schemes like the Lea Bank redevelopment, which are today rightly criticized for their excessive proportion of high-rise flats,[11] represented a very much better deal – socially, visually and in terms of new homes and open space only half a mile from the city centre – than the soulless edge-of-town estates being built by some cities.

Lea Bank today represents dramatically the turn of the conservation tide in Birmingham. Close by, Lea Crescent, a charming

group of small 1830s houses, faces downhill across the great green spaces carved out as a setting for the high-rise flats. It was to have been demolished. Instead it has been preserved and 'done up' and constitutes a superb foil and period 'leavening' to the redevelopment as a whole. The award-winning canalside rehabilitation at Brindley Walk by the City Council and British Waterways Board also represents a change of direction towards conservation. As Lewis Braithwaite says in his study 'Urban Canals' (*Built Environment*, June 1972): 'In many ways the towpath is as important as the water, for it provides the planner's dream of a segregated pedestrian network, and one, unlike most Inner Ring Road systems with their endless steps and urine-stained underpasses, on one level. And it is no dream. It exists today.'

The conservation tide is also running high in the central area, where the character of Birmingham as a fine Victorian and Edwardian city has belatedly come to be appreciated. The great bank and office buildings in Colmore Row and Bennett's Hill were ten years ago regarded as impractical Victorian monstrosities. Now (like London's St Pancras Station), they are cherished as survivors of a grand, full-blooded era. But the conservation area which has superseded earlier road plans round about Colmore Row, and which includes St Philip's Churchyard, also has its listed Regency buildings too – notably in the Bennett's Hill/Waterloo Place area, one of the earliest surviving parts of the merchant city. Though protected, these buildings still in many cases lack users willing and able to maintain them. A serious criticism of municipal policy is that its redevelopment strategy has tended to push out small specialist shops and activities without doing much to relocate them at rents they can

The city has recently had more success in finding developers willing to restore and convert Regency buildings in the Bennett's Hill/Waterloo Place area

afford. This looks like another example of the political/administrative disease of compartmentalism. The planning department says: 'We must preserve these buildings.' The valuer's departments says: 'We can only let them at current market rents.' So quite often they stay empty. The possibility of subsidizing a desirable user so as to ensure the 'lively preservation' of an attractive building does not seem to have been seriously considered.

Elsewhere, however, in the grandly Victorian Colmore Row, splendid late nineteenth-century office buildings are being retained and rebuilt internally within their sturdy, beautiful shells. This is not just because of their architectural merit, but because conservation is now cheaper than demolition followed by new construction.

1. Fergusson, Adam, *The Sack of Bath*, Compton Russell, 1973
2. A design by Leonard Manasseh & Partners was published by Avon County Council in August 1974
3. Cambridge has its development scars. They might have been worse
4. If development there had to be, then Owen Luder's new shopping block is, in my opinion, a creditable and sensitive attempt to 'fit in' with Bath. It is certainly a great improvement on the earlier shopping development to the north
5. Nairn, Ian, *Britain's Changing Towns*, B.B.C., 1967
6. Nairn, op. cit., p. 16.
7. *Drive* magazine, autumn 1971
8. The city has since made considerable progress in pedestrianizing city centre streets.
9. City Engineer, 1963–74
10. Jacobs, Jane, *The Death and Life of Great American Cities*, Pelican (reprinted), 1972
11. Lea Bank as redeveloped has a density of 153 persons per acre with actual building covering 43 acres of the site. Before redevelopment, people were packed into the old terraces at 171 persons per acre, building covering more than 86 acres

The Tyne bridges and quays form Newcastle's most exciting vista. The quayside area on the right contains some of the city's oldest buildings. Large-scale redevelopment on the hillside up to the city centre would wreck the dramatic townscape

The Bristol & West
Building Society's
headquarters rises
dramatically from
Broad Quay in the
city centre. If tall
buildings there had to
be, this was well
sited. But Bristol can
do with no more of
them. The C.W.S.
building (right) has
since been
demolished

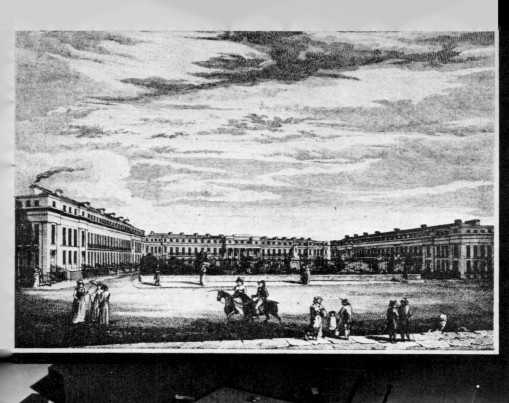

NEWCASTLE-UPON-TYNE is an under-appreciated town that has suffered much from development. The tide in favour of conservation has turned there now quite strongly: the new Tyne Wear County Council has a staff establishment for its conservation team, which will work jointly with the city and the other districts, of fourteen professional staff.[1] Its tough reactions to developers' proposals for sites in the city in 1973 and 1974 caused at least one property firm to say it could no longer operate in the city. In that particular case, the planners received this threat or warning with equanimity.

But in the late fifties and early sixties that was not the situation at all. The north-east of England, of which Newcastle is the effective if not nominal regional capital, was starved of development. The 'environment' (the word was not in vogue then, of course) had a run-down look. The function of town planning was seen there, as in many other cities, as the attraction of development and the creation by means of it of a bright, modern and efficient new world. Urban motorways would replace the congestion of outmoded city streets; 'fine' new office blocks and shopping precincts would bring a new diversity of jobs, aid prosperity and set new standards. That was what the people of the north-east seemed to yearn for. It was certainly how their political representatives interpreted their mood. The fact that some of the leading personalities of that era and a principal agent of the great reconstruction, notably T. Dan Smith and John Poulson, have since been jailed for corruption, does not invalidate the fact of its one-time popular appeal. Wilfred Burns, now the Department of the Environment's well-respected chief planner, was, as city planning officer at the time, the main agent of change.[2] But that scarcely lessens the seriousness of the mistakes.

Some of the results have, however, been horrifying; many more extremely disappointing, even to those who sought after them. In the former category undoubtedly comes the destruction of the greater part of the magnificent Eldon Square, by the city council itself which should have been its guardian, in the interests of creating a new shopping precinct. Eldon Square dated from 1824–6 and was the work of that architect/developer team who so profoundly changed and moulded Newcastle in the early nineteenth century, Richard Grainger and John Dobson. A superb three-sided square of stone-faced terraces, bringing for the first time to Newcastle the spaciousness and grandeur of Nash's Regency terraces in London (but without their ornament), this was the first planned expression in the city of its metropolitan ambitions. A sad irony, then, that not quite a century and a half later a new set of ambitions to revitalize Newcastle as a metropolitan city should have been so blind to the quality and importance of Eldon Square as to pull down two-thirds of it over the protests of local and national preservationists. That was in 1970. Five, even three years later, the conservationists' tide would have been strong enough to turn that decision the other way. The new shopping precinct would have had to be put somewhere else, even if, in 'planning' and commercial terms, west of Northumberland Street and north of the markets was the logical or 'optimum' location. Commercial development has a habit of protesting that it can only make a scheme pay on such a site, and will not build it elsewhere; then, when site x is firmly ruled out of court, suddenly discovering that site y is not only possible but has a number of hitherto unappreciated advantages. Going all out for commercially the best site is to be expected of developers. Grainger would no doubt have done the same. It is less easy to forgive a local authority for aiding and abetting them in the destruction of a prime piece of its city's architectural heritage.

One of the disappointments was Grainger's Royal Arcade, whose exterior Pevsner called 'noble and reticent'.[3] It stood in the way of road-building and redevelopment. Protests at its intended demolition led to a promise to preserve the interior in the midst of the new world of subways and tower blocks. The merits of this kind of preservation – a fraction of the original composition artificially retained but with their whole context and point destroyed – is very much open to doubt. In this case not even that happened. The architects, Robert Matthew, Johnson-Marshall (who were surely unhappy at what they were asked to do), found they could not save the arcade. It crumbled as they touched it. They ended up rebuilding its interior in replica, a beautiful but lifeless and synthetic fragment stranded at a draughty crossroads of underpasses and pedestrian routes beneath a huge roundabout. This is the dead, museum-piece approach to preservation. The Arcade would have been better remembered only in pictures, or if kept, relocated in more sympathetic surroundings. As it is, it is a mockery. And it is the kind of mockery to which large-scale redevelopment and large-scale urban road building all too often lead us.

One Newcastle disaster which illustrates damage to a town not so much by what is destroyed as what goes up is the Norwich Union tower at the bottom of Westgate where it joins Collingwood Street. Insensitive both in its size and its materials, it calls to mind the strictures of Sir James Richards, former editor of the *Architectural Review*, on the terrible damage this (commer-

Below: Norwich Union developments, said Sir James Richards in his 1972 R.I.B.A. discourse, have done unforgivable damage to the face of British cities and towns. Norwich Union building, Newcastle

Below right: Newcastle Royal Arcade – a beautiful but meaningless replica amidst a maze of pedestrian subways

cially no doubt admirable) firm have done to the appearance of so many English towns.[4] But it is also a monument to the pitfalls of letting commercial hunger control civic design. There can be argument about whether the Norwich Union's original proposals for this site (considerably lower and with a less unattractive finish) should have been permitted on so important a site. People would argue that a large modern building could never have come to terms with the Victorian splendours of Central Station or of the Georgian Grey and Grainger Streets round the corner. Others would say that a smaller building, forming a gateway to the street as this does, but less brutal in its line and more sympathetic in its cladding, could have succeeded. What in fact happened was that, after the city had agreed to the Norwich's first proposals, the company pleaded a change for the worse in the economics of the development. They could not go on with it without some increase in space and some reduction in the cost of the visual treatment. The city planning committee took the view that Newcastle could much less afford to lose the jobs and prosperity that office block represented than the luxury of a marginally better townscape. It seems that they would not take that view now. But the lesson was learned too late.

There is no lack of other visual and environmental disasters in Newcastle to drive home the lesson. The inner motorways now, as in other cities, undergoing a drastic rethinking, supply their share and sometimes prompt mixed feelings about otherwise admirable exercises in conservation. The seventeenth-century Holy Jesus Hospital, skilfully restored and converted in 1971 as premises for the John George Joicey Museum, is blemished by the harsh proximity, two or three feet away, of a new elevated roadway. Quite apart from the rush and roar of traffic, all that lovingly cleaned and repointed brickwork has as its neighbour the nasty slabs of aggregate cladding mistakenly employed by the road builders as fashionable cosmetic to their structures. Honest steel or concrete (especially if of high quality) would have been better; a road on a different line, preferably further out of town, the desirable answer.

But the new in Newcastle is not all disaster; and it would be unfair and unbalanced to pretend otherwise. The 1968 Civic Centre (by the City Architect, George Kenyon), though not as welcoming to the citizen as Sunderland's later equivalent, has managed to be both a symbol of Newcastle's postwar resurgence and in a real sense a popular landmark. It changes rather than damages the scene of which it is part, which now includes William Whitfield's award winning University Theatre – a poem in fine modern brickwork. In the town centre, Spence's new central library and adjacent buildings, whatever violence the

Proximity to an unsympathetic new elevated road ruins the setting of the beautifully restored Holy Jesus Hospital.

William Whitefield's University Theatre is a poem in well mannered townscape and (above) beautiful brickwork.

clearing of their sites may have done, have come to terms with the Newcastle townscape and provided public spaces at elevated walkway level which can be used, some Newcastle people say, with pleasure and without the wind-tunnel effects that so often frustrate the best intentions. Another view is that they are narrow, nasty and bitterly cold in bad weather.

Redevelopment (taking place at the time of writing) in the triangle running down from Bigg Market to St Nicholas Cathedral is more controversial. Many conservationists have complained that a fine vista of the cathedral is being wantonly destroyed. The city planners argue that St Nicholas will gain from tight enclosure of all save the tower with its 'crown' of spires. They seem to be arguing that there is something un-natural in having a vista here. Whatever the historical arguments, I think myself that this is a view that should have been preserved. When it comes to All Saints, however, the complex of low-rise, detached office blocks which have sprung up round that church seem to me to give it an admirable sense of enclosure. It is to be hoped, however, that the city will resist pressures to let this development spread down the hillside destroying the fine old lanes, alleys and warehouses and blocking impressive views of the Tyne Bridges. Newcastle planning today is like the rich merchant who has secured his fortune by questionable com-mercial dealings and can now afford to repent, be upright, and maintain a rigorous stance in defence of what remains.

Right: Newcastle's 1968 Civic Centre expressed the vitality and pride of the metropolis of the north-east

B RISTOL, one of the more attractive and historic of large British cities, was another place which only belatedly realized how high a price it was paying for redevelopment. The postwar start in rebuilding the blitzed Broadmead area as a new shopping centre was architecturally and in planning terms a great disappointment. Developers and traders resisted almost to the point of boycott proposals to create a traffic-free precinct there, and only the threat of an out-of-town hypermarket at Cribbs Causeway has provided the impetus, two decades later, for a scheme to pave over those streets and exclude cars.[5] Aesthetically, the redevelopment there was a foretaste of the kind of 'shoe-box' commercial architecture which functionalism, on a tight budget and with little sensitivity to existing townscape and local visual tradition, was to produce in so many towns.

Twenty years of such development in the historic centre of Bristol have done much damage. The Merchant Venturer tradition of commercial opportunism is still very powerful; and it is no coincidence that the leader of the city council for much of the later period of intense redevelopment, businessman Gervas Walker, liked whimsically to call himself 'a merchant' and seemed to many observers to be rather too 'entrepreneurial' in his attitude to planning control. That is to say, he looked upon development control, over which as chairman of the planning committee he exercised an often dominant influence, as largely a matter of commercial 'Realpolitik'. The principal agent of these policies was the then city engineer, who doubled as city planning officer and who ingeniously – and with an enthusiasm not shared by conservationists – sought to accommodate the motor vehicle, moving and parked, in the centre of the city.

The result of these attitudes and policies was intensely destructive. Part of the price was paid in the more ugly towers and slab blocks that are such ill-mannered neighbours to the smaller-scale mixture of medieval and sixteenth-, seventeenth-, eighteenth- and nineteenth-century buildings that previously made up the inner city. Partly it was paid in the swathes of destruction cut to make way for 'modern' high density roads, and in the kind of massive barrier, visual and psychological, of parallel carriageways, underpasses, walls and bridges that now separates the city centre and the Broadmead shopping area from what was once their natural extension, Old Market.

As to tall blocks, the dyke was breached by the Robinson paper group's building at Bristol Bridge. Though controversy raged about its size and design when it first went up in 1964, familiarity has now muted that criticism. It is a simple, elegant

block whose use of pre-cast concrete units has much to teach
many later exponents of that medium. The view of it from the
old city or from across the Floating Harbour is still exciting as it
rises sheer from the water. But it did open the flood gates. And
the flood included many mean, nasty and much worse-sited
buildings. We can do no more than look at a very few examples.

One which owes its existence and shape very largely to the
city planning department in its earlier, engineer-dominated era,
stands on the other side of the floating harbour from the
Robinson building, overshadowing the seventeenth- and
eighteenth-century King Street which the city has striven to
keep as a living museum of the Bristol of that dynamic and
stylish epoch. In Queen Charlotte Street, scarcely one hundred
yards from the eighteenth-century Theatre Royal and the
seventeenth-century Llandoger Trow Inn, rises a brutal bastard
of a building, which is in effect a tall office block superimposed
on a multi-storey car park. A developer wanted an office block
there; the city engineer (and planning officer!) wanted public

car parking. His simple solution was to suggest the one over the other. The result is an insult both to the skyline and, at street level, the townscape. In a part of the town where streets still, to their glory, have doorways and windows every few feet at street level, here is a dead expanse, an alien aggregate clad podium. Its lines, and indeed its main apertures, are horizontal in a vertical street scape. No faces look out; only, at awkward levels, the grills of motorcars.

Once such a policy holds sway, the results are hard to control. The most prominent of the new landmarks, the Bristol and West building at Broad Quay, is a feature that most Bristolians have by now come to accept, even to admire. But you cannot do with many – perhaps any – more of them. Across the wide expanse of 'The Centre', Bristol's Piccadilly Circus, has risen a second tower. As a building it is perhaps in some ways a more elegant construction than Alec French & Partners' Bristol and West tower. Its architects, Moxley, Jenner & Partners (who restored one of those early seventeenth-century King Street houses as their own offices), are deeply concerned with both the quality of new buildings and the conservation of old. Perhaps they would have been happier not to build on that site. So too no doubt would the present city planning officer. But the planning consent was given in the early 1960s. It could not be revoked without a crippling bill in compensation. Moxley, Jenner preferred to make the best of a bad job rather than see others perhaps make a worse job of it.

One of the worst blows to the overall townscape of Bristol was inflicted by the city council itself. Kingsdown, a hillside rising up from the River Frome opposite the quays of the medieval city, was one of the earlier suburbs – dating mostly from the 1760s or several decades before the bulk of Clifton. Its visual excitement came from a combination of very steep eighteenth-century streets running up the hill and terraces running along it. Much of this area was in decay, but that does not excuse the blockbuster of a municipal housing development the city lumped on to the side of this hillside in the early 1960s. It wrecked both the scale and the sense of stylish detail that comes from rows of thin 1760s houses with pillared and pedimented doorways climbing the contour or marching in orderly variety along the skyline. Too late the professional middle-classes tired of the northern suburbs and returned to restore and convert; too late the amenity lobby succeeded in changing the form of redevelopment and an architectural competition produced the tight-packed, urban two-storey housing of the High Kingsdown scheme. But already the bulldozer and the thick and nasty

Above: A tower block that got away – regretted by the planning authority before it was built – destroys the backcloth to the carefully preserved Orchard Street
Top right: The city's own battleship of a council housing development wrecks the hillside of 18th-century Kingsdown
Centre right: An out-of-scale office block dwarfs the tower of St John-on-the-Wall
Right: The backs of one of the surviving Kingsdown terraces, looking down on the city centre

aggregate-clad horizontal podium had destroyed the texture, at least in the distant view from the city.

By the end of 1973, it was clear that the tide had turned. The city planners (or enough of them) understood what conservation meant and how much they still had worth conserving. The former grandiose road programme had provoked such widespread opposition as to materially assist the defeat of Gervas Walker's Citizen Party and the election of a Labour city council pledged to stop the destructive Inner Circuit Road in its tracks. Under local government organization the city had, indeed, no direct control over roads and transportation, the responsibility for which lie with Avon County, where the same Gervas Walker was majority leader. But by then a combination of rethinking of transport policy by central government and severe limitation on public spending were already making it unlikely that the money would be available for road construction on this scale. An unofficial report by the independent City Docks Group[6] on the future of the city's extensive redundant docklands (which stretch right into the centre of the town and almost to the walls of the medieval city) provided another powerful argument for abandonment of the road plans. The dockland area freed from the blight of the proposed roads, argued this group of young professionals, could accommodate the equivalent of a new town of 10,000 people, living within

walking distance of the employment and recreation that the city centre had to offer. And this could be built in a varied, 'fine grain', low rise architecture recreating the lanes and alleys that Bristolians liked best about their city. The sterilizing effect of the proposed roads and interchanges on the central 'island' of the docks means less usable land, less employment there, fewer homes, and the need to screen people from noise, visual intrusion and fumes by building large 'barrier' buildings. These, incidentally, would be barriers to pedestrian movement and social activity as well as barriers to noise and visual intrusion.

That decision was, at the time of writing, still in the melting pot. Others seemed to be receiving more sensible, sensitive answers from the city planners than they would in the 1960s. Perhaps the turning point was the decision of the then Secretary of State for the Environment, Peter Walker, in the 1971 case of the Avon Gorge Hotel. The Minister there not only 'called in' for public inquiry a planning application on which the city had already given outline consent; but, on the basis of the inquiry inspector's recommendation, ruled against them and landed the city and its ratepayers with the cost of compensating the developer for an enforced revocation of that outline permission. The amenity lobby in Bristol received a great fillip; the Merchant Venturer approach to development control took a severe knock, from which perhaps it has never recovered.

Soon after this, the era of 'engineer's planning' in Bristol ended with the retirement of James Bennett, and development control within the city has shown a generally very much more sensitive touch. One disaster averted was a proposed new Post Office tower which would have risen 300 feet, again virtually in the back garden of the Theatre Royal, King Street. Happily the iniquitous Circular 100, which in effect allowed government departments and public corporations to ignore the wishes of the planning authorities when proposing new developments, had lately been superseded by a new Circular 80, which backed the duty to 'consult' with the ultimate sanction of a public inquiry if the local planners and the public sector developer could not agree. With the help of this lever, the planners (their resistance stiffened by sharp criticism of the scheme from the Bristol Civic Society and others) persuaded the Post Office to reduce its new central telephone exchange to a more tolerable six storeys.

The church of St John-on-the-Wall, at the end of Broad Street, is one of the few points at which you can still see that Bristol was once a walled city. The city fathers then were thrifty folk: the tower of the fourteenth-century church served also as fortified gateway, the wall of the nave is the wall of the town. Behind it

Above: The Granary warehouse, 19th-century Florentine, is a listed building with only half a use. Its lower floors resound to the sound of pop and jazz groups; effective conservation demands use of its upper floors but fire safety requirements make this difficult and expensive.
Below: Granby Hill, Clifton. Some of Bristol's more sympathetic modern infill

run narrow lanes, between and sometimes under later buildings. Two modern buildings on either side of this gateway, just inside it, show how much more sensitive and creative an instrument development control in the city has become in the last two or three years. Both buildings are by Alec French and Partners, designers of the Bristol and West tower. The earlier, to the south of Broad Street, is a great, grey-out-of-scale office block which relates neither to the church nor the street, and which in manner and materials is alien to its surroundings. (Almost the only point in its favour is that it arched over and preserved the back-of-walls lane.) On the north side of Broad Street, the same architects – nudged and cajoled in the right direction by a determined and creative development control officer – have done altogether better. Their Legal and General scheme is low-rise, low-key, and wraps itself round several worthwhile existing buildings. Instead of a brutal, blank podium, the wall of the development is full of windows, doors, recesses, courts, alleys and arcades, penetrating its line and breaking it up visually. The materials chosen – grey flint-lime brick and grooved, exposed concrete – may not be perfect, but they do not obtrude or clash. On the further, John Street side is a little square – planned for people, not cars – with attractive paving and two walled beds with trees and flowers. One tree, as a plaque attests, was placed there by his colleagues in memory of John Totterdill, the rank-and-file planning officer who coaxed and argued for many months to make this crucial redevelopment a more sympathetic and humane one. Alec French and Partners paid for that plaque. That act and the building itself are his own best memorial.

Elsewhere in the central conservation area, the city planners are achieving a remarkable degree of restoration by making this in effect a condition of redevelopment. Application to build office blocks at the derelict backland buildings of eighteenth-century houses in Queen Square more readily gain consent if the developers are prepared to keep and restore the houses, or at least their façades, or in extreme cases rebuild. Developers are also being persuaded to reverse the worst changes in façades, to clear forecourts of parked cars and reinstate railings. As to the new buildings at the back, the current guidelines to developers call for them to be designed as much like warehouses as possible. That, after all, is what was there originally; such buildings fit the waterside character of this wharf area; and current architectural thinking has belatedly come to the conclusion that a building of denser construction than curtain wall, with small windows to cut down heat loss and solar gain, is more economical in a time of rising fuel prices and fears of energy crises. One conservation technique being adopted by the city in this area commends itself as both practical and cheap. Waterside roads once tarmacaddamed over for cars are now being reinstated to cobbles. All this involves is a simple instruction from the city engineer not to replace the tarmac when traffic rubs it away. Eventually Queen Square, one of the grandest residential squares in Europe, but cut diagonally by a main road in the 1930s, is to be closed to through traffic and the road paved or grassed over.

1. But in the summer of 1974 the county was having considerable difficulty in filling many of these 14 conservation posts
2. Burn's view of the goals of Newcastle planning are to be found in his book *Newcastle: A study in replanning at Newcastle upon Tyne*, Leonard Hill Books, 1967. In particular, on p. 25 he writes: 'The proposed Newcastle Central Motorway System is sometimes on two and sometimes on three levels and with widths, including access and egress ramps, of up to eighteen lanes. It is clearly impossible with features such as this to try to ignore the road or attempt to hide it as being a civic design element that is unworthy of serious attention. *A finely engineered multi-level junction needs to be seen as an exciting new element to be added as a positive feature to the central area landscape . . .*' (my italics).
3. Pevsner, Nikolaus, *Buildings of England: Northumberland*, Penguin, 1970
4. Richards, J. M., Royal Institute of British Architects annual *Discourse*, 1972
5. At the time of writing, cars had been removed from Broadmead, but the streets not yet paved over. The imaginative scheme prepared for the area by Moxley, Jenner & Partners stood little chance of early implementation, apparently because of the unwillingness of traders to contribute financially
6. *The Opportunity of the Docks*, Bristol City Docks Group, 1974

Top left: How objectors saw the proposed new hotel on the Avon Gorge at Clifton
Top right: The new Legal & General development near St John's Gateway
Left: The developer who sought permission to convert and extend this house in Queen Square as offices was asked to restore its railings

Right: Northampton's market square: the heart of the town and the key to its identity
Below: Tamworth's new shopping precinct: horizontal façades and wide service roads destructive of the town's fabric and character

AMONG medium-sized towns brutally assaulted by re-development, Northampton is a sobering but instructive example. With a population in 1968 of 131,000, it stood at the centre of its county, a quiet though still prosperous market and manufacturing town. It had some notable buildings, but many more townscape and architectural delights not noted in the guidebooks and perhaps rather down-at-heel, though appreciated by the more discerning townsfolk. Northampton's earlier expansion to the 100,000 and beyond was associated with the growth and mechanization of the shoe industry.[1] Its current expansion results from designation as a 'new town': one of the 'partnership' towns in which a government-appointed development corporation and the local authorities together carry through the construction and other programmes needed to house a much larger target population – in this case to 200,000–260,000[2] by the 1990s.

The arguments here are complex and conflicting. Even with a decreasing birth-rate, the population of Britain continues to rise and the number of households rises rather more steeply. People's expectations of a reasonable home in a satisfactory environment demand not only housing redevelopment in existing towns but a substantial provision in new communities. The New Towns Acts with their apparatus of development corporation and planning and budgeting over decades rather than years provide admirably for this. The supply of houses they plan and build is not so much at the whim of the market or financial stringencies in the public sector as private or council housing. And, though sometimes criticized for late social and shopping provision, new towns have generally done very much better in their efforts to provide balanced facilities in time than most other developers, public or private.

New towns are, however, unpopular with many conservationists. Rural conservationists and farmers dislike them because they have traditionally taken green field sites – areas ranging in England from 2,000 to 22,000 acres, much of it prime agricultural land. Several of the so-called 'third generation' of new towns, designated in the 1960s and much larger in their planned populations, are not strictly 'new' at all. The strategy is to build new neighbourhoods on open land round about the existing town, with local social and shopping facilities but to gear up the existing central area to provide the bigger and better shopping and social facilities, as well as many of the jobs, required by the expanded town as a whole.

It is this central area redevelopment that in Northampton has done the damage. The showpiece buildings like All Saints, (rebuilt after the Great Fire of Northampton in 1675), the circular Holy Sepulchre church, the Sessions House (also 1670s) and the early nineteenth-century Repertory Theatre, are appreciated and avoided by the municipal developers. But set-pieces are one thing, townscape quite another. It is the lesser buildings, and above all the total picture and overall scale and character, whose importance the town council has consistently failed to appreciate. Demolition of a fine-textured townscape, full of little buildings, vertical division and interesting detail, has again and again been followed by construction of monolithic blocks, not so much tall as bulky and typically with wide horizontal bands of concrete or aggregate cladding. They are alien, and they impoverish the setting of the carefully preserved jewels.

A case in point is Haselrigg House, one of the few pre-Fire buildings, which has recently been restored and sensitively adapted by a local architectural practice as its own offices. It is statutorily listed. Other adjacent buildings were not, and were therefore vulnerable to demolition. The 'march of progress' can be seen at its worst further along and on the opposite side of the same street, Marefair, in the great slab-cake of a Barclaycard headquarters. Such a building, whatever its merits might be as a free-standing piece of architecture, has nothing to do with the traditional townscape of central Northampton or the quality and scale of this street in particular. If towns are conceded to have a character, then the Barclaycard building is one of the nastiest pieces of character assassination I have come across.

'If towns have characters . . .' of course they do, and they are more important than is generally realized to the ordinary people who live in them. Much of Northampton's character depended on the Market Square, which sustained a sad loss by the destruction of the seventeenth-century Peacock Inn to make way for (I quote Juliet Smith in her *Shell Guide to Northamptonshire*) 'a huge, out-of-scale supermarket adorned with olive green panels of dispiriting drabness'.[3] That was in 1962, and it led to the formation of a civic society which has since fought valiantly (and often bitterly) against the superior resources of a 'develop-or-bust' town council. 'But it could not happen now,' you say. Perhaps not. But what did happen only in 1972, over the loud and numerous protests of townsfolk from all walks of life, was the demolition of the late nineteenth-century Emporium Arcade – a key building in townscape if not architectural terms on the north side of the square.

The reason for the demolition was so that Grosvenor Estates could the more conveniently build a new shopping precinct on

land they owned on that side of the square. The arcade stood in the way of efficient, comprehensive redevelopment. The official view, expressed in Northampton Borough planning department and, in response to a 20,000-signature petition, by the Department of the Environment, was that its architectural quality was not sufficient to merit its retention. Only emergency 'spot' listing could have saved it at that stage – a device which the department's Historic Buildings experts use very sparingly and did not think justified here. A 1901 arcade with a brick clock-tower and Art Nouveau tiled façade was no doubt an interesting curiosity, but scarcely merited statutory protection.

Yet for Northampton's sake it should have been preserved. Its façade was not everyone's idea of beauty, but it had in

Above: The old Peacock Inn, one of the visual lynchpins of Northampton's market square
Above right: The undistinguished supermarket block which replaced it

seventy years become part of the square's character for almost
everyone who lived there. It had a distinctive personality, was a
key point of reference visually. The Civic Trust's award
winning film on conservation *A Future for Our Past* reminds
us: 'A town without old buildings is like a man without a
memory.' Northampton's memory, and sense of identity and
direction, have faded badly because of that demolition.

The town, of course, did need more and better shopping. But
Grosvenor could (and, I think, would, if pressed) have realigned
their scheme to take in the arcade, whose delicious galleried and
domed interior would at least have led somewhere as originally
intended. It would also have provided a continuing link with the
old Northampton and some mellow character to take the 'shine'

off the new development. One argument in favour of letting Grosvenor redevelop as they wished was notably a non-argument for anyone who knew the example cited. Look how sensitively the Grosvenor-Laing shopping precinct at Chester fits into the historic setting of the Rows, it was said. The Grosvenor-Laing precinct in Chester is indeed a credit to both city and developer. But the main point about its sensitivity is that it fits in behind existing façades and between buildings of character and quality. It is a very persuasive argument for Grosvenor to do the very thing they refused: build behind the façade and round and over as much of the arcade as possible.

One other and smaller building affected by the shopping precinct proposal was the pre-Fire Welsh House. The civic society (which, with Northampton Action Group, sought to save the arcade) were prepared to see this go. Its structural state was such that the fabric would have had to be renewed and what was left would be in reality little more than a replica, they said.

Above: The Rows at Chester. This row in Bridge Street and another in Eastgate Street (right), link directly into the Grosvenor-Laing shopping precinct behind. Here the Grosvenor Estate, because they had to, fitted successfully a shopping development behind the existing buildings

The arcade, though architecturally less special, was more important to the Market Square townscape. Perversely, the Secretary of State of the time, having given thumbs down to the arcade, ordered Grosvenor to keep the Welsh House; and they were obliged to redesign their scheme to do so. It will be the more interesting for that redesign – but it would have been infinitely more so with all or part of the arcade.

And to anyone who says that a developer's architect must have a clear site to produce satisfactory architecture, let me cite the opinion of a recent past president of the Royal Institute of British Architects, Peter Shepheard. Faced with this argument

Above right:
Barclaycard building, Northampton: 'toothpaste' architecture, which runs on along the street until a halt is at last called

at the Public Inquiry in 1970[4] into proposals for redeveloping Whitehall (involving demolition of Scotland Yard and Richmond Terrace), he produced what must rank as a classic conservationist counter-argument. The constraints of existing buildings which have to be kept on a large redevelopment site ought to constitute a challenge to the architect and, if he is skilful and sensitive, can result in a better architecture than a monolithic structure on a cleared site, said Shepheard. In an existing town, variety is what makes townscape attractive – and particularly English townscape, which more often than not shuns the monumental. The Shepheard argument would apply very aptly to Northampton. Perhaps there has lately been a change of heart; but if there has, in many respects it comes too late.

I have written here of only one of the two causes of drastic change on the face of Northampton: redevelopment. The other is roads. A point which ought to be made, since the town council and the development corporation have been mentioned as partners in the expansion, is that the two early agreed to divide their responsibility for implementation. The development corporation concentrated on building housing, local centres and roads in the expansion areas outside the existing town; the borough applied itself to building urban expressways and, with developers, promoting the redevelopment of the centre. It is the town council,[5] which ought to have been the main guardian of the town's architectural character and visual identity, which has been responsible for most of the damage.[6]

If Northampton is the medium-sized town wrecked by insensitive expansion, then Tamworth (1974 population approximately 50,000, twelve miles north-east of Birmingham) has a strong claim to be considered a prime example of the small town that suffered the same fate. In 1954 Tamworth was a small market town with a population of 14,000, a fine castle on a hill above the meeting of two rivers, and an attractive town centre grouped round its early eighteenth-century town hall: a compact and fine-grained townscape stretching from the foot of the castle mound to the fourteenth-century[7] parish church. No fewer than ninety-five buildings had been listed by the then Ministry of Housing and Local Government as worthy of statutory protection worth their historic or architectural importance. By 1971, thirty-six of them had been demolished and, incredibly, no conservation area had been designated nor, at that time, proposed.

What was the reason for the devastation? The *occasion* of it was the 'planned expansion' of the town from 14,000[8] to 80,000 by

Below: The junction of Lichfield Street and Silver Street as it used to be. Above: The same crossroads, with townscape, blown apart by demolition and the construction, set back from the old frontage, of six unnecessary tower blocks

Tamworth borough, Staffordshire county and Birmingham city councils under the Town Development Act. The *cause* one can only put down to failure to give sufficient weight to conservation and continuity in the life of towns. Here was a town that had been a town since Saxon times; it had for the most part grown gradually to a splendid maturity in Georgian and perhaps Victorian times. The twentieth century brought stagnation and the spectre of decline, and seemed to offer the choice (used as a slogan elsewhere by the Greater London Council's expanding towns division) 'Expand or Die'. But the initial study by Tetlow & Goss, though paying a certain lip service to preservation, chose the bulldozer's way. Like the official town map of 1969, it displays a frightening confidence that wholesale clear-and-rebuild will be better than repair-and-infill, that the provision of 'modern facilities' requires and justifies wholesale destruction; and that the preservation of odd set-piece buildings or small groups of buildings will somehow safeguard a town's character in the face of brash architecture alongside or a tower block at the end of the street.

Tower blocks there are – six of them, right alongside the main crossroads of the town – and quite good tower blocks they are, in isolation. Designed by Birmingham architects Mason, Richards & Partners set in an inner city location – they would probably have deserved an award or two. But in the centre of Tamworth, they are a crime on several counts.[9] First, why in a small town – and a small-scale town – put people in a fifteen-storey block of flats when they could live in houses with gardens or (if they prefer flats) in two- or three-storey blocks that do not dwarf the existing buildings. The castle and the church, for centuries the vertical features of Tamworth, should not have to compete with so inappropriate a skyline.

Secondly, there is the price paid in destruction and unhinging of the urban pattern. They were sited so as to destroy effectively the south side of Lichfield Street, formerly one of the finest Georgian streets in the country. Three Grade 2 (i.e. statutorily protected) buildings were demolished here, and four Grade 3 (not statutorily protected but which, in the climate of a few years later, would almost certainly have been added to the list). Round the corner in Silver Street, which leads to the river bridge, a whole row on the west side has gone. There the traditional street pattern and the townscape of a key crossroads have been blown needlessly to pieces. The street as it has existed for centuries has been jettisoned in favour of high-rise set back.

Right: Church Street as it was, companionable shops and right townscape. Opposite: The new Middle Entry shopping development, round a grey desolate square which, visually, 'leaks' in all directions. At least it's better when they hold an open market there

The town at this point as a result no longer holds together. This cannot be said of the new shopping precinct, which at least is fairly low-rise and makes some effort to 'slot in'. But at what a cost! Church Street in 1950 had twenty-five listed buildings. Now only thirteen of them remain. The five gabled shops which faced the church up until 1968 were the epitome of medieval Tamworth. Now we have a paved square (where they do at least hold markets) faced on three sides by indifferent commercial architecture that might be anywhere. One of those five gabled shops dated back to the 1400s and contained a nearly complete medieval hall and solar – a rarity which the town, and indeed the nation, should have cherished. Another had Tudor windows looking out on the street – again an irreplaceable feature of the street scene which should have been cherished, not demolished. These five gabled shops were all demolished in the space of ten short days in 1968. What have we got instead? The new, out-of-place Co-op building and other similar shops.

The town council's argument has been that an expanding Tamworth needed more and better shopping. That can scarcely be gainsayed. What is open to dispute is whether it needed quite so much, and whether all that destruction was necessary to make room for it. Lewis Braithwaite, extra-mural lecturer in Urban and Environmental Studies at Birmingham University, argues that (a) the amount planned is excessive and (b) that it was a fatal mistake to try to accommodate the bulk of it in the historic centre.[10] He notes that the first town draft map of 1954 envisaged growth from 14,000 to 20,000. It dealt extensively with the architectural and historical quality of the town and concluded that growth could be reconciled with retention of its historic character. The revised town map of 1969, looking to a popula-

The cathedral town of Lichfield has enjoyed the constant and well-funded attentions of conservationists and restorers. Its new shopping centre has been skilfully fitted in behind existing buildings; its listed buildings do not seem ever to have been down-at-heel like Tamworth's

tion of 78,000 by 1981, significantly had no section of historic and architectural character but seemed to be looking at the settings of individual historic buildings rather than at historic areas. Braithwaite concluded 'The county had written off Tamworth as a historic town.' It certainly seemed to many people to have taken a backward step to what I call 'pocket handkerchief preservation'.

Staffordshire's view of Tamworth's future was revealingly summed up by the then chairman of the county council, Alderman John Oxford. In a special Tamworth survey in the *Birmingham Post* on 11 May 1972, he wrote: 'The whole aim of applying the best and most up-to-date planning principles to this situation is to create an environment for people to live and to enable them to relate to the human scale in a pleasant and exciting town.' So far, so good. But then he gave the game away: 'Tamworth,' said Mr Oxford, 'should be transformed into a spacious town of the twentieth century.'

The climate now has changed a little. A few buildings will be saved and restored which were in danger. But the dead hand of insensitive planning still threatens. Market Street and what is left of George Street (nine out of eleven buildings listed in 1950 are now gone) are the subject of recent conservation and pedestrianization proposals. But the county planners still seem to be rushing in like well-intentioned bulls in a shop full of delicate china. If they are left to it, the result cannot but be more disasters. The price of pedestrianization is said to be more rear access roads. The precedent of such a road carved through the Church Street frontage is not reassuring. But have they not heard the news? Norwich and Leeds and a dozen towns in

Germany have found you do not need rear access to service shops in a shopping foot-street. Provided the pedestrian clearly has the upper hand, vans and lorries can come and go at walking pace and still leave the street essentially pedestrianized. Or else, if the streets are too narrow, deliveries to shops can (as at Norwich) be 'trolleyed' over the paved footstreets from the nearest unloading point. And then there is the unbelievable plan to cut a road between George Street and the Castle mound, destroying the gardens and attractiveness of the George Street houses and the tranquillity of the mound at one stroke. It is not needed, it is not wanted. And it could be fatal. For conservation is more than propping up structures. It is giving buildings new life. This could happen in Tamworth where, as at Lichfield, living at the hub of an attractive and historic little town could become a healthy fashion. But not with unwanted roads shaving back gardens of historic seventeenth-century houses, ruining the best vistas and bringing traffic noise and fumes to the very walls of the castle and its adjoining park.

So though Tamworth may not be a bad town to live in as modern towns go, it is a great loss as historic towns go – and a great deal of it has gone! A changed approach on the part of town and county councils can still rescue something worthwhile in the way of character and atmosphere. If there is no such change, then Tamworth will steadily and inevitably become what Lewis Braithwaite sadly protests it is already: 'Brumworth' – or Birmingham writ small; 'Tetlograd' – a monument to planners who dreamed of a brave new world but were blind to the quality and potential of the down-at-heel old one. You only need go the seven miles to Lichfield to see what might have been.

1. Postwar growth to around 130,000 was to a large extent the result of borough boundary extensions
2. Growth to 200,000 is by 'planned' growth to 1981, and to 260,000 by 'natural increase' thereafter
3. Smith, Juliet, *Northamptonshire: A Shell Guide*, Faber, 1968
4. *The Times*, 30 July 1970
5. Northampton was a county borough until local government reorganization in April 1974
6. In April 1974 Labour-controlled borough and county councils took control and announced cancellation of the Expressway project, while apparently disagreeing on which of them should take the credit for the decision. The county is the roads and transport authority
7. Parts are earlier, but most dates from rebuilding after a fire in 1345. See Pevsner: *Buildings of England: Staffordshire*, Penguin, 1974, p. 275
8. Some apparent population growth is due to boundary changes
9. Pevsner calls them 'visually fatal and functionally, in terms of a town of this size, unnecessary'. Op. cit., p. 278
10. Braithwaite notes that if all the town centre redevelopment schemes before the Ministry of Housing and Local Government in 1966 had been carried out, England and Wales would have had enough shopping provision for 164 million people!

5 FAREWELL, LONDON: VANISHING CITY

LONDON is probably the place in Britain where the collision of profit and sentiment has been at its worst. I use both terms here in as neutral a sense as possible. It is in a commercial sense natural, and certainly not in itself reprehensible, for property owners and users in a large capital city where commercial activity is increasing, to want to 'renew'. They seek to replace offices and hotels built in the nineteenth century and the early decades of the twentieth century with larger and more efficient office blocks and hotels. They seek to replace collections of small buildings on small plots by larger and supposedly more efficient buildings on big plots. Preservationist and public opinion may regret such changes for a variety of reasons. Some people may regret almost all change. They are temperamentally ill-equipped to stomach the loss of the familiar. They may at the other end of the scale regret the loss of, or threat to, individual buildings of exceptional quality, either in architectural or historical terms. The destruction of Hardwick's Doric arch at Euston Station (which Pevsner calls shameful[1]) or of Bunnings Coal Exchange in Lower Thames Street, 1962 (which he calls stupid and unnecessary[2]) have both ingredients. We may regret the demolition of old buildings of no special architectural quality, but which fitted in scale and character, and their

replacement by new buildings which are sympathetic in neither respect. They are bad neighbours to the good buildings which remain. Again we may deplore the destruction of 'the street' by buildings which are set back from it, face at right angles to it, or otherwise fail to relate to the shape and feel of it. On the other hand, we may be reconciled to, or pleased with, certain new buildings in their close setting, but regret what they do to the skyline or the distant view.

But beyond and transcending these 'visual specifics', many people feel a wider discontent which has taken much longer to find expression. It is that redevelopment, even if architecturally decent, can erode or destroy the character of places. Perhaps we may pick out two factors here. One is the sense that a district, a neighbourhood, should have a distinctive identity: familiar, memorable, providing visual signposts. The other is the sense of lively mixture and human scale which people associate with such places and which, with a few honourable exceptions, are missing in new development. A final factor is the pace of change. This is one aspect of a thesis which will be familiar to many readers from Alvin Toffler's book *Future Shock*.[3] Individuals and societies can assimilate a certain amount of change in their environment at a given time, depending on circumstances.

Right (both pictures):
The Coal Exchange,
which the City
Corporation insisted
on demolishing
against all argument
in 1962. They then
left the site empty for
years, disproving the
alleged urgency of
demolition

Right: Despite loud
and reasoned protests
from preservationists,
British Rail, with
government approval,
destroyed Hardwick's
Euston Arch. A
legend persists that
its pieces are stored
somewhere in London
Above: The waiting
hall of the old Euston
station

Beyond that point, disorientation sets in with both mental illness and social alienation among its by-products. This is examined a little further in my final chapter. Suffice it to say here that, in the fifties and sixties, there was in London too much change too fast and on too large a scale for most people to absorb. One result has been a weakening in people's sense of association with places. They no longer relate to different parts of London as they did, no longer identify them or identify *with* them. The constant lament is that new buildings and developments are so alike and so anonymous. That complaint is partly, but by no means entirely, justified. The truth is that we are most of us suffering from a chronic attack of visual indigestion.

The area where change has been most drastic, and the conflict between profit and conservation most acute, is probably the City of London. Commercial interests and the City Corporation have, in the name of the twin gods of utility and economics, wrought more destruction of fine buildings and streetscapes than all the bombers and flying bombs of the Second World War achieved. The skyline here is the great overall loss. It used to be relatively low, punctuated by the spires of Wren churches and a few other vertical features such as the Monument. Over it all the dome of St Paul's asserted an effortless dominance. That is gone. Church towers and spires are now submerged in a sea of curtain-wall office buildings. You now have to search out Wren churches hidden in crevices between the commercial slabs. If you approach the city from the north along Farringdon Road, you at first ask yourself: what is that odd rectangular façade with an elegant dome sitting uneasily on it? The answer on closer inspection is: an office block which from that angle hides the entire cathedral *except* its dome. From the heights of Greenwich Park, the once wonderful view of the city is now a forest of tower blocks. You have to search out a diminutive St Paul's. The city is no longer separate but its tower blocks merge into those of the West End. The dominant vertical now (of its age an exciting and appropriate one) is the Post Office Tower. Both the City Corporation and the G.L.C. have taken pains to preserve sight-lines of St Paul's across and along the river, and with some success. You can mostly see it, but it isn't the same dominant feature in the skyline. As the towers of Mammon have grown taller, not only St Paul's but the spires of the other Wren churches seem in relation smaller. The landscape – and the people in it – have been shrunk.

From almost countless cases in the City of handsome or sympathetic buildings destroyed and replaced by ugly or out-of-character ones, a few examples must suffice. Parnell's National

The City as it used to be, seen from the Monument. St Paul's is the dominant feature; Wren spires rise effortlessly above the office blocks

Westminster Bank in Lombard Street, demolished in 1963, was a rather grand five-storey building in Italian *palazzo* style. It and a fine neo-classical building next door were grand banking halls in a street of grand banking halls. They had character which people walking past could mentally catch hold of. The replacement, by Mewes and Davis (once, when the original Mewes and Davis were alive, the authors of many distinguished buildings), is seven storeys, decent but utterly unmemorable. In Bishopsgate, Baring's Bank, in red brick by Norman Shaw, and its neighbour by Horsley, one of his pupils, were modest in style but added a richness to the townscape. They were demolished primarily because of road widening plans which are daily less and less likely to be realized. Another example of a poor swap was the demolition of the albeit mutilated Sun Life building in Threadneedle Street (mid-Victorian by Charles Cockerell) for a new Sun Life building, which is so bland and featureless that it clubs that part of the street almost into insensibility and destroys the vista along Royal Exchange Avenue.

Some people attack the City's London Wall and Barbican developments in the north of the 'Square Mile'. There is indeed a certain amount of man-made desolation in the office blocks and windswept elevated pedestrian ways on the new London Wall. But redevelopment did least destruction to the London Wall/Barbican area because it had already been to a great extent flattened in the Blitz. Opinions differ about the two rows of office towers that line London Wall. Some find them banal; others (and I tend to agree with them) regard them as an exciting vista. It is closer to that the visual quality breaks down. And it is at least arguable that most of the city might have been preserved at something like its old roof level if the bulk of new development could have been concentrated in that area to the north with many more towers of the London Wall kind. With hindsight we can see that it is possible, given the present climate in favour of conservation, to persuade commercial concerns to keep attractive old buildings in conservation areas as prestige offices for small central staffs, with the bulk of office work accommodated anything from fifty yards to two hundred miles away. The pity is that a combination of commercial conservatism and vested interests in high land values appeared at the time to rule that out of court. Those vested interests were incorporated into planning law with a bonus of permitted development beyond mere replacement and modernization. It was to some extent these so-called 'Third Schedule Rights',[4] and the practice of expressing development permissions as 'plot ratios',[5] that wrecked Wren's skyline.

Conservation and redevelopment as sympathetic neighbours in the Barbican

St Paul's from Farringdon Road, its dome all but hidden by an intervening office block

View up Threadneedle Street to new (pitched roof) Sun Life building and (inset) the old Sun Life building on the same site

Another cause for regret quite out of proportion to the merits of individual buildings demolished is the fate of the stretch of riverside between Blackfriars and Southwark bridges. Here were the old commercial wharves of the City which first made it prosperous. Even five years ago, though the buildings had changed, it kept its medieval pattern: narrow lanes running between tall warehouses and providing dramatic glimpses of the river, its passing traffic and the higgledy-piggledy townscape of the Southwark bank beyond. Now it is utterly destroyed. What we have instead is the kind of comprehensive road-and-buildings redevelopment that architects and planners have been saying for years ought to be achievable. The dual carriageway is walled in (and often roofed in) in concrete; new buildings (including a school and a new telecommunications centre as well as a hotel and offices) are rising beside and in some cases over it. New broad pedestrian routes are being cut down from St Paul's towards the river. It has all taken some imagination and a good deal of persistence to achieve. Elsewhere it would gain more applause than it does. The regret comes from the loss of what was there: not just history, but the drama of that old quarter of warehouses and wharves. The new wide vistas are no substitute for the sense of enclosure of the old alleys and lanes, and the contrast when these opened out at riverside stairs. A good new hotel at Queenhithe is only very partial compensation for the loss of a handsome riverside warehouse that could have been incorporated as splendid public rooms in the new hotel; and the loss of part of the area, and much of the character, of the little square behind.

On the credit side, it must be said that a new highway in concrete cutting and tunnel away from the riverside is infinitely to be preferred (if road there must be) to a road like the Blackfriars underpass which scrapes the river embankment and leaves people on foot a riverside walk made thoroughly unpleasant by noise and fumes and rushing traffic. The redeveloped zone will eventually have a continuous riverside walk away from the road, weaving interestingly in and out of waterside buildings. Indeed one of the few sections of the City's pedway systems of which one can wholeheartedly approve has been inserted in a new riverside block on this stretch. At present it leads nowhere much, but this is surely one stretch of pedway that can and will be completed, with undoubted popular approval.

The unfinished pedway system is in a curious way a political tidemark. Odd sections of it crop up throughout the city, the high-water mark of a tide of comprehensive redevelopment that is now strongly on the ebb. The twin towers of one of the better

Battered Blackfriars! Left: Wren's St Benet's surrounded by new roads. Below: A cosmetic touch of nominal 'landscaping' between the Thames and the four-lane, traffic-bludgeoned canyon of Blackfriars underpass

Right: Ivory House, beautifully restored centrepiece of St Katharine's Docks. It contains shops, restaurants, a sailing club and service flats. Below: The interiors are lavish, though the architects had to use some ingenuity to achieve satisfactory daylighting to all rooms without altering the shape of window openings. They made unglazed window apertures open on to patio-balconies, which in turn light the rooms (Architects: Renton Howard Wood)

Below right: Demolition men quickly discovered that the brick walls of G warehouse disguised this very much older timber-faced building, originally a brewery. It has been moved on rollers to a new site, and after restoration will house a pub and restaurant. In the foreground is a retractable footbridge by Thomas Telford

office developments of the 1960s, Gollins Melvin Ward's P & O and Commercial Union buildings with their piazza between, are somewhat marred by it. The pedway leaves a dead floor near the bottom of the Commercial Union tower. The architects did not want it; their client did not want it; and it leads nowhere. It probably never will. The turn of this particular tide is shown even more graphically in Old Broad Street, where a bridgehead of the pedway system points eastwards across the street, poised to cut into a range of buildings most of which are now listed or officially proposed for listing. Not that listing necessarily protects against all comers and in all circumstances. Far from it. But the history of this site suggests that here the tide was stopped for good. Much of the wedge between Old Broad Street and Threadneedle Street was owned by National Westminster Bank who, early in 1972, sought permission to demolish a number of listed and other key buildings. Their architect, Mr Robin Seifert, argued that the Victorian and early twentieth-century bank buildings were (a) not up to much, architecturally and (b) lacked modern facilities like rear servicing essential to today's motorized and computerized banking. The City Corporation, supporting the development, added that the existing buildings were at a 'nodal point' in the pedway system. And whereas its elevated walkways can be inserted without too much difficulty into new buildings designed with that in mind, it would be difficult or impossible to run it through Victorian, Edwardian or similar buildings, at least without drastically affecting the façades for which they were mainly listed.

National Westminster and the City did not, however, have things all their own way. London is, in this respect as in many others, legislatively a special case. The G.L.C. has overriding powers on historic buildings, and perhaps the largest and ablest team of historic buildings experts in Britain to guide and support the exercise of these powers. They opposed the grant of listed building consent and thereby forced a public inquiry. Their witness, John Earl, produced detailed evidence that a key building, 51–3 Threadneedle Street, was not (as Mr Seifert alleged) only a poor imitation of a *palazzo* in Rome and an example of a peculiarly weak and imitative period of British architecture. The building, by Arthur Davis[6] and dating from 1927, was, he said, a strong and rather splendid example of the commercial-classical style then in favour among bankers. It had won prizes in its day, and been highly regarded by architectural authority then and since. He would, he said, like to see both sides of Threadneedle Street preserved, including buildings not intrinsically important; and he would extend his preserved

townscape round the corner of the wedge into Old Broad Street.

That was the battle of expert testimony. But anyone with a halfways sympathetic eye could see what he meant. Threadneedle Street comprised a harmonious townscape, all to scale and all of a style. There were tower blocks to be seen if you craned your neck, but at street level it still worked visually. The street had not been wrecked by lumpish podia or intrusive access roads, at angles to the street, destroying its homogeneity. And it was more than just a *cause célèbre* for architectural historians. Thousands of city workers knew this street, felt it elegant and easy on the eye, in their daily comings and goings. It was one of the best remaining complete chunks of the vanishing city of forty or fifty years ago. For that as well it ought to be kept intact. As I wrote at the time,[7] if the Secretary of State for the Environment let them get away with that, then 'Good-bye to almost all the City's familiar scene. Conservation there will have been degraded to a mini-pocket handkerchief affair. Crude economics will have beaten the heart out of it.' But he did not let them get away with it. He refused listed building consent and

The City Club, which a proposed new tower block for National Westminster threatened with destruction and which the Department of the Environment at first refused to protect. They have now 'spot-listed' it

broadly accepted the arguments for preserving the Thread-needle Street townscape as a whole. And in 1974 he went one stage further than the G.L.C. Historic Buildings men had expected. He listed a building they had reluctantly (but I think wrongly) written off: Philip Hardwick's City Club, dating from 1834 – as attractive in its way and full of character as almost any Pall Mall club, which Mr Seifert had counted (reasonably, in view of past Ministry attitudes) on having down without hindrance or opposition. The spot listing in June 1974 must have come as much of a shock to him and his clients as it was an unlooked-for delight to the conservationists.*

So there stands the pedway bridgehead, pointing at a row of buildings most of which have been either so to speak 'preserved by public inquiry' or the subject of recent and emergency 'spot listing'. That is why one doubts if it will ever go any further. If I were the City Corporation, I would put in an escalator or two and bring pedway firmly down to earth.

In some areas the City has recognized the strong feeling among its huge working population in favour of preserving the small-scale lanes and streets where, as mid-day shoppers and lunchers, they enjoy strolling. One such area is at Bow Lane, where the city planning committee took an unwontedly strong line in resisting out-of-scale development proposals. For the first time they here made use of the 'Section 8' procedure under the 1972 Planning Act which allows designation of buildings not meriting historic building listing as 'key' buildings whose demolition requires special consent. (It was also presumably to be the last time. The Town and Country Amenities Act 1974 makes all demolition in conservation areas subject to planning control.)

An area where the fight is still very much on is in the block north of Throgmorton Street and Lothbury, north-west of and at one corner touching on the Old Broad Street/Threadneedle Street wedge already mentioned. This area has a few indi-vidually worthwhile buildings, but its quality again rests on intimacy of scale and the attractiveness of a complex of alleys and lanes which weave through and round buildings. Nowhere has the City Corporation or any of its developers convincingly shown that such urban character can be sympathetically created in new development. The charm of byways like Angel Court† and Throgmorton Avenue comes from the piecemeal nature of their development, a patchwork of ages, styles and heights and widths of frontage. The best small-scale infill can honour their spirit. It can scarcely ever replace or enhance. Large-scale redevelopment in the City has almost always destroyed that character. Sometimes, like Commercial Union and P & O, it

* An appeal was later lodged
† Now demolished

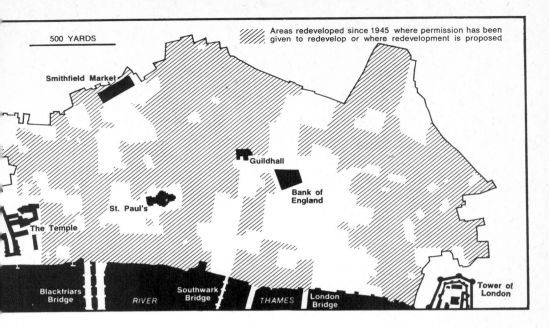

has a personality of its own one can respect or even warm to. Mostly it is anonymous, banal – a net subtraction from one's sense of place.

Areas of the City redeveloped or threatened with redevelopment between 1945 and 1972

The accompanying map was drawn in the autumn of 1972. It was based only on development that could be seen or proposals for development which were public knowledge (and generally had planning approval). The shaded-in area covers about two-thirds of the City of London. It was not then excessively greedy or unreasonable of conservationists to argue that the rest should be looked at very carefully to see whether it had anything worth preserving before sanctioning even more redevelopment. And that, in one or two places, is the way things have been going.

Take, for instance, the Carter Lane area south-west of St Paul's. Its fate is to a large extent bound up with roads, and recent damping down of road-building activity has helped. But the main tale to be told here is of stiffening public resistance to large-scale redevelopment. Originally to be redeveloped comprehensively, this area, like Bow Lane, has a strong character derived from a mixture of mainly eighteenth- and nineteenth-century buildings erected by past developers on what is basically a medieval street pattern. Its roads twist and turn, are punctuated by alleys and churchyards and courtyards, pubs and corner shops and archways leading to such hidden oases of calm as Wardrobe Place. Here as elsewhere the City Engineer has been trying for years to widen the narrow streets. Replacement buildings had to be 'set back', like teeth knocked out of the row;

and the replacement buildings were at best quite a bit taller and usually (in their materials and horizontal rather than vertical emphasis) not good neighbours. The official argument was that wider streets in these areas were needed to cater for increased servicing traffic. Yet in fact one of the attractions of the Carter Lane area, where road widening has not for the most part happened, is that there is room neither for more traffic nor for what traffic is there to move at much more than walking pace. Public opposition to change here seems to have killed specific proposals such as redevelopment of one side of Wardrobe Place (refused by the city planners after protests from tenants and office workers). It also appears to have achieved abandonment of the city's own 'preferred strategy', which sought to be a mid-way solution, but involved some damaging road widening and quite a large chunk of new building between Carter Lane and St Paul's Churchyard. The Corporation now seems to have accepted a 'minimum change' solution which will spare both the grand, grim Victorian office buildings that are such a good foil to the cathedral on that side, and the corners the City Engineer would have knocked about, including part of the Dean's garden.

The cavalier nature of that official's attitude to historic buildings when road schemes are at stake is well illustrated by his action in 1973 in slicing off a large triangular chunk from the nave of a bombed Wren church, Christ Church in Newgate Street. Somewhat taken aback by the strength of public protest, the City protested in a rather pained way that they had secured all-round agreement to the scheme a decade or more before; that they planned to create a 'quiet' garden inside the diagonally walled-off nave (with the full weight of diverted traffic pounding past); and that the alternative was to run the road across a site the Post Office owned and had for twenty years been promising to redevelop. The spokesman I talked to seemed to find nothing odd in his masters' preferring to run a road through a Wren building rather than a public utility-owned bomb site. It was, after all, cheaper. And that is how the City of London reasons. But it should not be too aggrieved if others think differently.

There are three last areas whose fate is still on the face of it uncertain. First Leadenhall Market, a lofty-roofed Victorian structure in brick and iron and glass. I do not call it a building because it is a pattern of streets with market shopfronts roofed in in grand Victorian style and connecting with lesser alleys and lanes. The City Corporation, who own it, have looked after it superbly, and since its most recent repaint, with the cast-iron columns in rich purple, it looks really splendid. It was designed

Above: The City Corporation sliced its road through the corner of Wren's Christ Church, Newgate Street; but (below) they have now been persuaded not to destroy the picturesque streets of the Carter Lane area south-west of St Paul's

and built in 1881 by a former City Architect and Surveyor, Sir Horace Jones; but the corporation would like to chop a slice off its western edge to accommodate a long-plotted road widening. They should not be allowed to. Leadenhall Market is too good to be thus ruined (and it would be ruined, for much of its quality depends on a sense of spaciousness and completeness in its cruciform ground plan). The road scheme is anyway otiose, and seen by most sensible people so to be.

Second, the Port of London's Cutler Street warehouses, which lie between Bishopsgate and Aldgate off Petticoat Lane. Begun in 1782, by the East India Company, these splendid buildings span the whole history of warehouse construction and goods handling from that date until Victorian times. The Port of London Authority, of course, wants a good commercial price for the site, and so is not much taken with the notion of preservation. The warehouses ought to be preserved, and used. Restoration should (as will be needed) be massively subsidized from the public purse. And if the user is some public body like a university or museum, then conversion and running costs may have to be subsidized. The subsidy will be more than justified.

Third, the area north of Billingsgate Market (itself soon to be redeveloped), between Eastcheap and Lower Thames Street. Full of the little lanes and alleys and passages of an ancient trading quarter, it is one of those small patches that ought to be kept for its overall character and texture as well as individual old and interesting buildings. The block west of St Mary at Hill has been ruined by ill-mannered development; but Lovat Lane, Botolph Lane, Botolph Alley and Church Cloisters need protection and skilful, but not excessive, attention. Now that the old lanes and wharves between Upper Thames Street and the river have largely vanished, this other area of remaining original character off Lower Thames Street is the more valuable. It was here that City fortunes were first made. Today's City can spare more than a thought. It can afford to keep a few streets, if for no other reason than to remind itself of the foundations of its present prosperity.

1. Victorian Society annual report, 1961–62
2. Pevsner: *The Buildings of England:* London 1, Penguin, revised 1972, p. 187
3. Toffler, Alvin, *Future Shock*, Pan, 1971
4. Now 8th Schedule to the 1971 Town and Country Planning Act
5. Plot ratio is the amount of floor space allowed in relation to the size of the site
6. Of Mewes & Davis, in name the same firm which designed the vista-destroyer critized on p. 72
7. *The Times*, January 1972

6 LONDON
GOODBYE, PICCADILLY

Previous pages:
Piccadilly Circus with
the Criterion Theatre
behind Eros

Below: Architect
Dennis Lennon's
design for a new
building alongside the
retained theatre
façade

THE destruction of the old City of London causes a more acute regret because it was a concentration of fine buildings and the Square Mile. The scale of Colonel Seifert's and other people's blockbusters injures (whatever trouble they may take with materials and fenestration and the like) because it is in such contrast with the tightness of the City's fabric. In the West End the effect is more diffuse and therefore less damaging overall; but when we come to particular cases it is often just as grievous.

I have called this chapter Goodbye, Piccadilly, because to many people Piccadilly symbolizes the West End of London, and because the struggle that has gone on for years there to prevent the developers' and the road engineers' worst excesses in some ways symbolizes popular distrust of large-scale re-development and illustrates its strengths and weaknesses. But this chapter looks at the West End generally, and indeed the areas south of the river which have come to be treated as 'West End'. It is not, of course, a comprehensive review. That would require several volumes rather than one chapter. But it does, I hope, pick out some significant examples and draws some useful conclusions from them.

The Piccadilly story is indeed a remarkable one. Between 1958 and 1968 no fewer than six full-scale plans for the redevelopment of the Circus and its environs were put forward either by developers who owned much of the land or by public authorities or by the two acting in concert. The first, in 1958, was a master plan from the old London County Council. It foundered basically because it had insufficient support from the land-owners and potential developers. Then in 1959–60 came Jack Cotton's development-for-profit plan which provoked intense opposition and led to a public inquiry. Presiding over that inquiry was a Ministry inspector called Mr (now Professor Sir Colin) Buchanan, who even then· showed the awkward independence of mind which has since made his a famous (if not always universally applauded) name. In recommending rejection of the development, he said in his report to the Minister: 'Piccadilly Circus attracts people from the ends of the earth as it is, and if comprehensive redevelopment is to take place, then it should be to a standard that really justifies a journey from the ends of the earth.'[1] The Minister agreed with the public and his inspector: the Cotton plan did not justify such a journey. It did not get built.

Then followed a series of other plans which sought to reconcile various conflicting pressures: for high quality of development; for profitable use of expensive sites; and (at least in the 1960s and early 1970s) for more road space. There was: 1961–62, Holford Mark 1 (one level); 1964–65, Ministry of Housing plan; 1966, Holford Mark 2 (two level); and 1968, various developers' architects in co-operation with Westminster City Council. More than one local politician staked his reputation to some extent on ending the Circus's drift into decay by securing an acceptable redevelopment, and failed. More than one pronounced 'The public wants action', only to discover that a vociferous public detested the kind of 'action' proposed. The turning point was a seventh scheme in 1972, worked out by the city council and developers and claiming to have avoided some of the worst mistakes of the 1968 scheme. It would, claimed the city planners, keep both the developers and the pedestrians happy, while all the cars, taxis, vans and buses calculated by the traffic engineers ran merrily below the raised pedestrian decks.

The city council in announcing the new scheme in May 1972 pushed for early approval. It would rejuvenate the area while retaining its traditional life and vitality as a great and busy international meeting point, said the official brochure. Mr Hugh Cubitt, leader of the council, hoping that the project could go forward without a public inquiry, warned that the alternative was the area's decay into a 'neon-lit slum'.

The reaction to the scheme was, however, almost uniformly hostile. There were too many offices, too much traffic, the new buildings were too big, and an 'exchange of land used' between the Circus and Victoria Street, on which the scheme depended, was variously attacked as 'dubious' and 'unfair to shareholders'. But root-and-branch criticism can be seen as being of two kinds. One concerned traffic, congestion and pedestrian access. The inclusion in the scheme of two hotels of 500 bedrooms each and (at a conservative estimate) an extra 1,250 office workers, as well as car-parking for another 500 cars, all patently ran counter to policies of reducing the strain on central London. It was all very well for Mr Cubitt to point out that the Circus sat above the interchange of two underground lines, but shop and office workers who had to use them at peak hours could be forgiven for doubting whether (even with improvement and enlargement of the sub-surface concourse) public transport could cope with the additional pressure. The notion of Eros and his aura being picked up and relocated on a deck above the traffic also failed to appeal. People were almost as suspicious of high level decks and walkways as they were of subways. They wanted to be on the

Berwick Market, the heart of Soho. Small shops on the ground floor under the long new building have helped it keep its intimate character

'ground' and did not see why they should be pushed around to make room for traffic.

The second line of root-and-branch criticism concerned the nature of comprehensive redevelopment. On this scale and with these amounts of money involved, it would be destructive to the real liveliness and variety of land use in the area, said the critics. Even discounting the effect on rents of imminent redevelopment, too many of the existing kinds of users would be priced out of the market. It was not neon lights and good architectural design that made the area come alive, but the variety of shops, cafes, clubs and services which would probably not be 'economic' in developers' terms but gave the area its attractiveness and usefulness to Londoners and visitors alike. There was special concern for the 'soft' area east of the Circus and merging into Soho, where the Chinese community had relocated and thriven after another kind of redevelopment had driven them out of Limehouse. Another strand of opposition centred on the Criterion theatre which was threatened (though the west side of Lower Regent Street, Swan & Edgar and the County Fire Office were not). The loss of theatres in London was at the time causing increasing disquiet, and the threat to one more was as much a rallying point here as the potential loss of an attractive and characterful building. Critics of the 1972 plan also made the point strongly (and it holds good for much redevelopment elsewhere) that it was not lack of rebuilding that had made the Circus and its environs run-down and tatty. It was planning blight. Owners do not spend much on buildings which may have only a year or two's more life.

Well, despite all Mr Cubitt's talk of there being no need for a public inquiry, and dark mutterings from City Hall that this 'might be the last chance', the Secretary of State (after noting the growing storm-clouds) declared that there must be one. And in the face of near-universal hostility, the city and the developers withdrew and announced they would try again. They did, and the results were better. In December 1972 they produced a number of 'options' ranging from a high degree of redevelopment to minimum change. There has been much argument about the nature of the alternatives, with a 'fifth option' canvassed, put forward at a discussion meeting held at the Royal Institute of British Architects in January 1973. But the crucial difference between all the alternatives and the schemes of preceding years was that one impossible requirement had been removed from the brief. The demand of a 1965 government working party that the Circus should cater for 50 per cent more traffic had been dropped. Without the extra traffic, the need for pedestrian decks largely disappeared. Without pedestrian decks, public authorities could contemplate smaller scale development, since developers' profit margins no longer had to be large enough to pay for the decking.

At the time, I described Alderman Herbert Sandford, then chairman of Westminster's special Piccadilly Circus sub-committee, as 'like a mariner suddenly freed from the dead weight of a seven-year-old albatross'.[2] But Mr Sandford's thinking had also been transformed in another way. He had been one of a small party which had visited Zurich and Munich to look at underground concourses, and it had opened his eyes to the difference between the inadequate drainlike subways at Piccadilly and the spacious provision of wide, well-lit concourses with shops and cafés which both Zurich's Bahnhofplatz passage and Munich's Karlplatz concourse show are possible. Zurich's Bahnhofplatz concourse, though a shade clinical to English eyes, thrives underground, with a restaurant and a bank as well as twenty-six varied shops all doing a very profitable trade. Instead of Piccadilly's rabbit burrows down from the street, it has easy and attractive access with seventeen escalators and wide, well-positioned entrances to help.

Perhaps this was one factor in jolting Westminster out of a rut. Their new nervousness of a distrustful and potentially hostile public opinion certainly helped in producing the (at the time of writing) latest scheme of October 1973. Office content was reduced from 559,000 sq. ft. in the 1972 proposals to 335,000 sq.ft; the amount of space devoted to entertainment increased fourfold, and shopping also expanded. The scheme saw pedestrians and public transport as benefiting from any setbacks in building lines rather than general road traffic. The Criterion Theatre and the façade of the building were also saved, and the architect concerned, Mr Dennis Lennon, has since produced designs for an arcaded building alongside to the east which catches the spirit and scale of the Criterion without aping it in detail. There was, at the time of writing, still opposition to redevelopment plans for the Circus, but the developers and public authorities had moved perceptibly away from the large-scale, clear-and-rebuild-all-at-once towards 'piecemeal renewal' – something that had originally been anathema to planners. More and more it is realized that gradualism works better. Not only does each chunk of renewal have time to settle down visually, but so do users and tenants of premises. There is no sudden, large-scale eviction, but rather an extended period of adjustment. The altered economic climate of 1974 may be good for Piccadilly Circus. With the steam gone out of property development, gradualism and conservation of what we have may be the order of the day. That rather than the best laid schemes of town planners and architects, may 'save' Piccadilly.

Elsewhere in the West End, as in the city, tower and slab blocks have wrecked the townscape and parkscape. Though the tall tower blocks permitted on the margins of Hyde Park/Kensington Gardens are still few, they have changed the sense of scale and insolation. As individual buildings, many will find them admirable. Sir Basil Spence's Knightsbridge Barracks tower of 1970 is, I personally think, an elegant and well-mannered building. It does, to apply one of Sir Basil's own favourite analogies, 'belong to the right blood group' in relation to the red brick squares and terraces to the south. The London Hilton, which caused such controversy when it was built in 1961–63, may now even be regarded with affection if not with respect. But the overall effect of these and three or four other towers is to change the nature of the park. In the 1950s you could stand in the park, at least in summer, and imagine that countryside stretched endlessly beyond the fringe of trees. No buildings were visible beyond. Now they are, and they are tall. The illusion is destroyed. Landscape architecture had given Hyde Park limitless horizons; tower block architecture took them away, and shrunk the landscape. The park is still a fine and enjoyable place, but not the asset in visual and psychological terms that it once was.

Spence's Knightsbridge Barracks tower rises above Hyde Park. Though intrinsically an elegant, well-mannered building, it is one more rupture of the park skyline

But worse atrocities were perpetrated by tower and slab blocks badly sited elsewhere. We have already seen how views of St Paul's from the north are distorted almost beyond recognition by superimposition of office blocks. There are similar cases in plenty in the West End. All Soul's, Langham Place, which Nash designed as a pivotal point to turn his street and end his vista, is now in townscape terms robbed of its virtue by the brutish and bulky slab of a B.B.C. extension which should never have been allowed, even at half that height, in that position. Nash's circular portico with its sharp spire above stands out now not against the skyline or even against a jumble of roofs and skyline, but against a wall full of windows. Not only should the planning authority not have allowed it but the Corporation, which makes some claim to be a patron of the arts, should not even have proposed to maul so badly the arts of architecture and townscape.

Similar effects are produced by the siting of the Euston Centre towers to destroy the vista behind Holy Trinity, Marylebone; and the effect of the three huge and bulky towers of the Department of the Environment on both the Houses of Parliament as seen from the South Bank and on what is in other respects one of conservation's great successes, the restored St John's, Smith Square (now used for concerts, recitals and meetings). It is one of the great ironies of redevelopment that the D.O.E., a department of state created specifically to safeguard the environment, should be quartered in a building which has done more to destroy the London skyline than probably any other building.

The Euston Centre, mentioned above, though architecturally it may not wholly be without good features, stands as a warning against the results of maximization of office space on an unsuitable site. The buildings are alien and, to the pedestrian, unapproachable. A street with houses and shops has been replaced by huge walls of glass fenced off by trafficscape. You do not wander into the Euston Centre or arrive there by accident. Only by conscious effort can you reach it or penetrate it. The total effect in scale and arrangement, materials and surrounding roadways, is of a place where people do not matter and scarcely belong. If London begins to suffer from the American disease of 'urban alienation', much of the blame must fall on Euston Centre and other places like it.

One of them I would nominate (though strictly speaking it falls within the chapter on what our modern 'Highwaymen' have wrought) is Vauxhall Cross. What was a few years ago a place with an identity, a local centre, has now become the largest and most complicated roundabout in London: acres of

C extension as
al background to
Souls. Right: The
ton Centre as
kcloth to Soane's
rch at Marylebone.
tom: The
artment of the
ironment's unholy
ty of slab-blocks
John's, Smith
are, right
ground)

direction sign gantries, traffic lights, intersecting tarmacadam and barren triangles of concrete on which intrepid pedestrians occasionally take shelter. Rarely was there an environment so hostile to the pedestrian. Even the footbridges are exposed, off-putting and difficult to use. The traffic lights are all phased so as to speed vehicle flow and, incidentally, cause the maximum amount of waiting and subjection to traffic fumes to anyone on foot. The only real refuge is in the new Victoria Line station and its (nonetheless frustratingly incomplete) system of access subways. Life on the surface is no longer tolerable.

If the Euston Centre shows the dire environmental effects of maximizing office space, then Southwark Borough Council's sixty-acre Aylesbury Estate in Walworth is a dire warning of what can happen when the number of new homes built is seen as the sole or dominant yardstick of progress. It consists of slab blocks eight storeys high, maisonette piled on maisonette, with single blocks stretching sometimes 200 yards without a break. The homes inside are well designed, and are utter luxury by the standards of many of the families who moved into them, as I discovered when I went knocking on doors there in the autumn of 1970. Many of them came from the worst of the old Walworth tenements or from terrace houses in multi-occupation. Mrs Rita King, a warehouseman's wife, told me, for example: 'There we had an outside toilet, no bath and I had to boil every drop of hot water in kettles or pots. No, I don't think the estate's inhuman or bleak.' Nor did Mr Albert Ford, who lived in the same block. He thought his three-bedroom maisonette 'marvellous' and the supposed bleakness of the site mostly due to the continuing construction work on the 2,400-home estate. When a Tory councillor called Aylesbury Estate 'dehumanizing' and 'a concrete jungle, just not fit for people to live in', a spokesman for the Labour-controlled council retorted: 'People who move into it from tenements would laugh at such a criticism.'

They did. And in a sense they were right. Where there is a long housing list and people in real slums and in overcrowded conditions, the pressure is strong to turn homes out like a sausage machine by industrialized building, chopping the string of concrete sausages only where a road or a corner demands it. But the critics were right too. It does look inhuman. And if the householders were delighted in 1970, many of them – and certainly their children – are less so now. As that Tory critic Mr Ian Andrews, argued, it should have been split into smaller units, even if that meant lowering the density. Which is what Southwark now does. The borough is unlikely to build any more Aylesburys. It has learnt to make most of its public housing

Terraces or slabs? Southwark's Aylesbury Estate dwarfing the little streets that remain as its neighbours. Most local people have little doubt which they prefer

94

more human-scale, both vertically and horizontally. And industrialized building, which was officially in vogue in the late 1960s, is now not so and is used generally with much more caution. The temptation, when you have installed a powerful sausage machine on site, is after all to go on making sausages. The machine dictates the design. That is not (and especially not with housing) a good way of renewing the urban fabric.

Perhaps with hindsight, and with the benefit for house finance and machinery improvement, we would now do differently: keep and rehabilitate many of the old streets of terrace houses with little gardens, demolishing and renewing only selectively. The nominal 'housing gain' in numbers of new homes would probably be less; the contentment and sense of belonging would almost certainly be greater. But even when you do redevelop a large area at high density, it need not be so

hostile and forbidding as Aylesbury. This is shown most vividly by Westminster City Council's Lillington Estate in Pimlico, by architects Darbourne & Darke. It is built at a density of 200 bedspaces to an acre, which is rather higher than Aylesbury Estate in Walworth; yet there are no windy access balconies, no long drab corridors and barren lift lobbies, and nothing that most people would recognize as a 'council flat'. Instead, every home has a front door opening on to something you can recognize as a street, lane or alley. Sometimes these foot streets are in reality four storeys up from ordinary ground level – but they feel as if they are on the ground. And this is deliberate, because Darbourne & Darke believe almost as an article of faith that people need and should have close visual and physical contact with ground level spaces. So at Lillington 40 per cent of all

Darbourne & Darke's Lillington Gardens estate for Westminster City Council. Densities are comparable with those on the Aylesbury Estate, but everyone lives on or near the ground

homes are at true ground level and have a private space (garden or patio) of about the same size as developers of £25,000 spec suburban terrace houses offer their prospective owner occupiers.

Lillington, then, was designed so that all families with young children would be at ground level. What of the remaining 60 per cent of homes? If you came out of one of their front doors having been taken there blindfold, you might well conclude that you were in a lane of one- and two-storey houses, traffic free and whose householders took a pride in tending tubs and boxes and baskets full of flowers and shrubs. It is patently a place people feel happy and secure in. In fact you would be in what partner John Darbourne calls a 'roof street', three or four storeys up from 'the ground'. The fact that many visitors do not at first believe Lillington is a 'council estate' is both a compliment to the architects and an indictment of a system and a society in which people assume public housing will somehow inevitably be drab and visually sub-standard – that it will have, so to speak, an environmental 'mark of Cain' on it. This estate, in a comfortable, dark-red brick, is in tune with older brick buildings across Vauxhall Bridge Road to the east and with Street's robust Victorian church, St James the Less, whose character and position in the townscape it respects. Through a careful scaling down of roof heights, even the nave of the church rises above the new buildings. The importance of Lillington's human scale in townscape terms can also be seen from the way in which existing mature trees stand higher than the new buildings and its scale matches almost exactly the stucco terraces to the west. Socially, it is also a healthy place. Few people go to Aylesbury Estate unless they live there or have to. It does not invite people to wander through it. It is a vast 'block' psychologically across that chunk of London. Lillington, though it has no through route for vehicles running through the site, boasts a network of lanes and footpaths that are attractive to follow and take the outsider as well as the insider where he wants to go. And built into the development are three pubs and some shops. Lillington is no ghetto. Conversely, the surrounding area offers many well-established facilities that Lillington residents can reach on foot or by only very short journeys by public transport. It knits in with the London that was there before; and it is only sad that blindness and pressures of mechanical rules and cost yardsticks have prevented its lessons from being applied more widely than they have been.

1. Quoted in *The Architects' Journal*, 26 April 1972
2. *The Times*, 15 December 1972

Previous pages: Most
famous yet perhaps
least typical of
London villages:
Chelsea's Kings Road

T has often been said that London is not so much one place as a collection of places, each with its distinct identity and sense of place: a city of villages. The characteristic was brought out well by a Danish architect and Anglomane, Professor Steen-Eiler Rasmussen, in his classic 1930s study *London, the Unique City*,[1] and has since been penetratingly developed in relation to the suburbs by Nicholas Taylor in *The Village in the City*.[2] But it is true not just of the suburbs, but of inner areas too; and in some of these the previous attribute of urban sense of place is desperately under threat.

Much has been written of the destruction of Bloomsbury. London University has been rightly and frequently, but mostly after the event, criticized for tearing the heart out of Georgian Bloomsbury. That battle is, alas, largely lost. But it has lately served to focus attention on another and in some ways unique urban village of mostly later architectural vintage: the few blocks of Bloomsbury that lie between the British Museum and Bloomsbury Way, between Bloomsbury Square and Bloomsbury Street: the proposed site of the new National Library. When the project was first mooted, Victorian buildings (of which this area chiefly consists) were less fashionable than they are now. The British Museum, then the library authority, could be forgiven for thinking that their architectural importance would not override the powerful case for a new library building – the desperate need for which is scarcely contested. Successive Labour and Conservative governments have indeed listened to the objections to development on this site and pronounced in favour of the scheme. But this is one that refuses to lie down!

And rightly so. For this little chunk of Bloomsbury is what London is all about. It stands for the spirit and character of real urban places which should be the point of urban conservation quite as much as the preservation of listed buildings. It is a place which works and which people identify and like. It is full of book shops and cafés and homes – a 'lively mixture of uses' in a very real and present sense, not as an optimistic statement of planners' hopes or intentions. The University, apart from destroying many fine Georgian terraces and squares, has laid a dead hand on much of Bloomsbury. Large impersonal buildings spread across the area like a forbidding presence. The university 'campus' is recognizable and architecturally alien. It is continually saying to outsiders: 'You are not wanted in this part of London.' It has gone far enough. University people and users of the British Museum and its library find relief in the remaining areas that are *not* institutionalized. And, of these, the proposed library site is the most important.

The fight has, I think, been partly based on a sense of this, but has proceeded mainly on other grounds. The Camden Borough Council has resisted the scheme also on grounds of loss of cheap housing (though the library authorities now argue that their latest scheme would contain more housing); the G.L.C.'s Historic Buildings Board has argued for preservation of individual fine buildings including the Museum Tavern opposite the British Museum's main gateway and houses in Great Russell Street, Museum Street and Coptic Street. The character they have long had for countless Londoners and users of the museum was pin-pointed by the board in October 1973 when it formally asked the Secretary of State for the Environment to 'list' the more important buildings as of special architectural or historic interest. 'All these buildings,' said the board of the stucco-fronted Museum Street buildings, 'apart from their visual qualities, represent what appears to be part of a deliberate mid-nineteenth century policy of refronting in a Parisian style.' The

Museum Street — Bloomsbury south of the British Museum: a village of booksellers and small specialist shops threatened by proposals for a new National Library

rather taller buildings opposite the museum's main entrance are a later expression of the same tendency, and their red-brick Victorian-Parisian façades are a perfect foil to the monumentality of the museum courtyard and portico; their Parisian-Bohemian atmosphere the natural obverse of the hushed and disciplined world of books and bookworms to the north.

The G.L.C.'s request to the Secretary of State, still not answered by July 1974 – nine months later – was in a sense a gauntlet flung in the face of Ministry listing policy. Under pressure of public opinion, the D.O.E. had moved in the space of a very few years from a very sparing listing policy to, in the review of London listings, what was sometimes a surprisingly lavish one. The high water mark came in Covent Garden where, in announcing his decision on the G.L.C.'s redevelopment plans in January 1973, the Secretary of State simultaneously announced the listing of a staggering 250 additional buildings. But in contrast – and against the professional judgement of at least some rank-and-file historic buildings experts – the department studiously refrained from listing any new buildings on the library site. This seemed to some people strange and sinister.

For the D.O.E.'s recent policy, as displayed in Covent Garden and elsewhere, had been to 'list' even if it seemed probable that development would justify eventual consent to demolition. The application of that rule should surely have meant listing the best buildings on the library site. In spite of all the hard-won battles about planning control over crown developments, was the public developer, in the shape of the Department of Education and Science, being treated differently from the private developer? Was someone in the D.O.E., at ministerial or official level, determined that the national library project should not be impeded or embarrassed by one more complication and its attendant likelihood of a public inquiry?

The project at the time of writing seems to have been postponed for at least another year by economies in public spending. Late in 1973 the National Library authorities, anxious to give the other side of the case, showed me round the grossly overcrowded and inadequate premises of the present library. Their plight was dire, and the danger of serious loss of morale and difficulties of recruitment if a new building is not soon started, are considerable. Nor does the new building, by St John Wilson, promise to be as unsympathetic as many have feared. Neither of these factors, however, in the least destroys the overwhelming case for *not* building it on the Bloomsbury site. The arguments for putting it there (as distinct from the arguments for putting a new building somewhere) seem to me to rest on academic special pleading. It should be within reasonable range of the University and the Museum, yes. It must be next door or we are impeded in our scholarship – no! Many people could never understand why academics were too short of breath or time to take a ten-minute tube or bus journey to the kind of alternative site Camden or the G.L.C. were suggesting. But in fact now a much more attractive possibility has emerged. Mr Rippon's clamping down of an overheated Covent Garden redevelopment, assuming it is maintained by his successors, offers the possibility of making a new National Library one of the few large new buildings permitted there. It would fit in well with the new policies of minimum change and mixed uses proposed for the area, would put library users within walking distance of the museum and much of the university, and would bring substantial benefits to both areas. *

Other 'villages' in the centre would certainly include Soho (perhaps itself to be regarded as a collection of villages), the Charlotte Street area west of Tottenham Court Road and north of Soho, and parts of Chelsea round the King's Road. This last case shows very clearly that preserving buildings and ensuring

* A site at Kings Cross has since emerged as favourite.

103

Lexington Street,
Soho: a lively
mixture of uses.
Consent for
redevelopment was
refused

an 'economically viable' use does not ensure the survival of an
area's character or its usefulness to residents. The lament now
from residents in the streets around King's Road is that it has
become too much of a commercial success. Boutiques and
restaurants have taken over almost to the exclusion of the useful
corner shop or ironmongery. Like people in many other parts of
London, those who live in Chelsea are haunted by a recurrent
nightmare in which they walk through streets full of trendy
clothes shops and expensive eating places (or, in other cases,
less trendy clothes shops, secretarial agencies and hi-fi stores)
looking in vain for somewhere to buy nails, or lemons, or a pint
of milk.

   In this context, the promise that redevelopment will be 'to
scale' and contain a mixture of zoned uses is sometimes not

enough. The tenants of an attractive eighteenth- and nineteenth-century block of houses and shops bordered by Lexington Street, Broadwick Street and Beak Street in Soho were certainly not convinced by their landlords' arguments to that effect. The block, which has a pleasant intimate scale that distinguishes so much of the original Soho, contained the houses of sixty people, five cafés, a pub, and a variety of small shops and tailoring workshops. The landlords, the Sir Richard Sutton Settled Estates, sought permission to demolish and redevelop, permission to demolish being required because some (though by no means all) of the buildings were listed. But it was the whole block that the tenants and other objectors were concerned to save. They argued that redevelopment would threaten the homes and livelihood of a significant number of people and would continue the steady erosion of the character of Soho by small-scale redevelopment after redevelopment. This erosion they saw as visual, economic and social. The lower paid were being ousted from both homes and jobs in central London, to their detriment and the detriment of a healthy social mix in the areas affected. What the landlords proposed was a mixed development including homes, shops, offices and light industry. Offices were a new use, presumably regarded by this family trust as a more profitable one. But in other respects would the new 'mixture' be a gain or a loss to the area? Would numbers 47–53 (odd) still be a barber's shop, a painter, a small tailor and a family café? Would those tradesmen, or others with similar standards and prices, still operate in the block? The tenants doubted it. The rents after redevelopment, they were convinced, would be too high for the likes of them. The small workshops above or behind many of the shops were also thought to be vulnerable. Instead the tenants proposed rehabilitation of the existing houses, for which they were generally willing to pay reasonable increases in rents. They won the support of M.P.s and peers and of that indefatigable defender of old London, Sir John Betjeman. And in the end they won a victory. Westminster's planning committee refused permission on the grounds that the kind of facilities and employment that this block contained had indeed been too much eroded in the West End and ought to be protected.

A major difficulty with such belated changes of heart on the part of planning authorities (following, it must be admitted, belated public awareness of what is at stake) is that they may some years before have given outline planning permission, or even detailed planning permission for redevelopment of a kind which then seemed acceptable, even desirable. It may now seem monstrous and antisocial, but that does not invalidate the planning permission. Revocation of consent can cost large sums in compensation to the developer or landowner. The importance of the new and more liberal policy of historic building listing in this connection is that no compensation is payable simply because a building is listed which you planned (and had permission) to replace with something more profitable. And there is no appeal against listing. The opportunity for appeal arises only if you make an application to demolish the existing building and the planning authority refuses it.

Until July 1974, one way round this for the determined or unscrupulous developer was to let the listed building decay. Though in theory the local authority could order you to do the work or alternatively carry out works, these were limited to keeping the building wind- and water-tight. Though in theory it could compulsorily purchase, by an anomaly of the then law, compensation was based on its value not as a building which must be preserved but on the value of the site on the false premise that this was developable. Thanks to the Town and Country Amenities Act,[3] prepared by the Civic Trust and piloted through parliament as a Private Member's Bill with government and all-party support, this is no longer the case. Logic is restored, the anomaly reversed, and a planning authority can compulsorily purchase such a building at the much lower 'existing use' value. It can now also recover from the owner the cost of emergency repairs to an unoccupied building.

It is, however, doubtful whether this quite legitimate conservationist device to reduce the scale and impact of redevelopment as well as protecting fine old buildings, will be enough to counteract the destructive forces of long-plotted comprehensive redevelopment. I have mentioned the Charlotte Street/Fitzrovia area. Other parts of the district bounded by Oxford Street, Tottenham Court Road, Euston Road and Great Portland Street have considerable charm and something of the same small-scale, intimate, mixed use character. And there are threats in the area not only from private development, but also from public authorities, notably the Middlesex Hospital. There is a strong case for telling medical, educational and other authorities that they cannot expand on such in-town sites at the expense of cheap housing, small industry and the liveliness and convenience of the corner shop. Replacement, yes; but expansion, no. If decentralization is right for offices, then it is arguably right, on planning grounds, for hospitals and colleges. Some hospitals have, indeed, like Charing Cross Hospital, moved further out. Consultants with Harley Street practices may find it less convenient that way, but they are infinitely better equipped to cope with change than many of the humbler citizens ousted or adversely affected by redevelopment. And though the community may gain better hospital facilities, it loses seriously in other ways when the social and environmental fabric of the inner city is subject to such ruthless surgery.

But enough of villages in the central area. Familiar places with a character and identity of their own have also been savagely handled in the inner and outer suburbs. I must confess to being a little torn in my sympathies in one respect. There is much in planning terms to be said for the strategy of setting up counter-magnets to the immense pull of central London. And in order to create those counter-magnets for shopping and office employment, you need some redevelopment. Thus though the Croydon of the 1960s and 1970s, with its forest of office towers, its fly-overs and car-park blocks and new shopping precincts, is anathema to many conservationists (and by any reckoning, very ugly), I cannot bring myself altogether to condemn it. For all its faults, it is a recognizable place! And in functional (though not visual) terms, it does seem to work.

The tragedy of the suburbs is, for the most part, that the fashion for conservation came too late. In district after district, pleasant, unsensational but distinctive shopping streets were bulldozed and replaced by supermarket and multiple trader shoebox architecture that might have been anywhere. Just as 90 per cent of the package hotels in the average holiday brochure look alike whether they are on the Costa del Sol or in Bulgaria, so the shopping developments of the 1950s and 1960s largely look the same whether they are in Bristol or Birmingham, Chippenham or Carlisle. Streets of nineteenth-century houses, modest but potentially attractive Victorian squares, were callously pronounced 'unfit' or made the subject of compulsory purchase orders so as to produce what were on paper better homes in marginally greater numbers, but were all too often alien and unfriendly places whose creation destroyed communities and whose nature encouraged vandalism and all manner of anti-social behaviour and social malaise. With hindsight we can see that little houses with backyards may, if skilfully and systematically rehabilitated, make more acceptable homes than five-storey slabs with windswept access balconies and unusable landscaped surroundings; that existing shopping streets can be pedestrianized successfully without elaborate and destructive rear access roads; and that a shrewd mixture of selective renewal and rehabilitation can often keep and enhance the scale and sense of place, avoid harsh change and have the best of both new and old.

Croydon, 'village' of
tower blocks,
underpasses and new
shopping precincts
(inset)

But for two decades at least, this lesson was not understood. As Walter Bor, sometime president of the Royal Town Planning Institute has put it,[4] architects and planners 'over-concentrated their efforts on too many costly and over-ambitious schemes . . . (there was) too much wholesale redevelopment of housing to the destruction of cohesive communities'. Large parts of the East End show this all too clearly. In contrast to the dull but human-scale (and now mature and spacious) acres of the G.L.C.'s Becontree Estate, the effort and ingenuity of the 1950s and 1960s was put into building towers and slabs to provide hygienic homes for workers to meet as quickly as possible the depressing large housing waiting lists. The streets they replaced often merited demolition, but not always. Too much that was attractive and eminently improvable was swept away. The surviving streets and squares (for example, the early nineteenth-century York Square in Stepney) survive not necessarily because they were the best, but because by chance they were late in the redevelopment schedule. The bulldozer was switched off before it reached them.

And you can see in some places where it stopped. In Islington, the borough council's large Packington Estate, all decks and upper walkways and service roads, marched across St Peter's parish eating up the streets. One charming little square that stood in its way was Union Square. Amid protests, it gobbled up half of it, then ran out of momentum. One half of that square is 'deck architecture' in concrete with aggregate panels: the other half is much improved and appreciated Victorian terrace houses. They have gardens or backyards of their own, and they please the eye. The new Packington to most people does not.

Union Square was a place, and indeed the area about, now that the tide has turned, still keeps some of its village quality. Despite the hazards of gentrification (and, in some ways, because of the new middle-class leavening), Islington has many neighbourhoods with that quality. Buildings, of course, do not make it; but the wrong kinds of buildings can prevent it from ever existing. A sense of place, visually, can exist in what would once have been considered the most unpromising places. One of my favourites, Boundary Estate, in Shoreditch, consists of artisans' improved tenements built in the late nineteenth century to replace one of the worst and most notorious East End slums.[5] They are tall, rather gaunt dwellings, but built round a circus with a little raised circular garden and bandstand in the centre. You could mistake this place, Arnold Circus, for nowhere else in London. Its trees are now mature and, visually at least, it must be regarded as a distinguished environment. A combination of

Above: Union Square, Islington: half a Victorian square destroyed and replaced by brutal, out-of-scale public housing
Right: Alwyne Road, Canonbury: unnecessary redevelopment prevented

Above left: New Islington council flats turn a sympathetic face to Camden Walk

Above: This key corner house in Wilmington Square, Islington, was too decayed to save. The borough architects rebuilt two façades in replica, with functional flatlets for old people behind them

Far left: This façade, newly built with functional old peoples' flats behind it, was designed to 'pay respect to' the Islington street of which it is part

Left: Gardens and courtyards at Lewisham's Evelyn Estate at Deptford are enlivened by pictures drilled on brick screen walls. This one depicts the Russian imperial eagle. John Evelyn's diary tells of the visit of Tsar Peter the Great to Deptford's dockyards

internal improvements (new bathrooms and kitchens, knocking three flats into two, perhaps) and enhancement of surroundings, including exclusion of through traffic, can convert such places into attractive environments physically. Arnold Circus is now, happily, in a conservation area and its buildings listed. The *rond point* of its terraced, tree-planted mound with its vistas from the radiating streets is, therefore, reasonably safe from demolition and redevelopment.

Another place where the tide turned late, and only because of ministerial fiat, was in Hackney. The borough's policies there showed very much the blind-man's-buff symptoms of clear-and-rebuild described above. Against this background of long housing waiting lists and desperate housing need, councillors and officials went all out to secure the maximum number of new council homes even at the expense of pulling down street on street of sound, attractive little houses, cherished by owner-occupiers and tenants. Mapledene, an area of 1840s' and 1850s' terrace housing in the borough's Dalston area, was such a case. The houses were set in wide tree-lined streets, each house having its own (by modern, public housing standards) generously sized garden. Hackney council wanted to demolish these houses and redevelop at a slightly higher density with local authority flats. Its planning consultants pronounced that the area was 'at the end of its useful life'. But 'useful' is, in this context as in others, an extremely subjective term. They also claimed it had no architectural merit. But that is a subjective question too. The residents (who were not a gentrified middle-class enclave like parts of Barnsbury, but a socially very mixed though stable community, took a different view. They forced a public inquiry on Hackney's compulsory purchase orders, and the Ministry inspector, Mr Donald Kearsley, declined to swallow the council's and its consultants' bland dismissal of Mapledene. He thought the area attractive as it was, and estimated that it had at least forty years' useful life ahead of it – probably more. As to the quality of housing that might result from improvement, the consultants had put it at 60 per cent as good as that achievable by redevelopment. The inspector assessed it at 90 per cent, and added: 'If some people thought that too low, I should not be surprised'.[6]

The Minister accepted his inspector's findings, refused to confirm the compulsory purchase orders, and stopped Hackney council in its tracks. Blight was lifted from the area, and the way opened for improvement. There was plenty to build on, visually and architecturally, as *The Architects' Journal*[7] has shown. But that is not perhaps the main importance of the Mapledene decision. The physical and visual qualities are perhaps less important than the turmoil and individual heartache involved in tearing down and rebuilding. You cannot easily quantify the costs of uprooting hundreds of families and dispersing a settled community. And Mapledene was and is a settled community. Many councils are not good at taking account of that kind of factor. It involves value judgements, and in general officials tend to prefer to tot up pounds and pence, or points on a supposedly 'objective' scale of the physical fitness of buildings. The objectiveness is often questionable. Call an area a slum, blight it with the threat or promise of redevelopment, and it becomes curiously much easier to label individual people's homes 'unfit'.

The message of this chapter is that Hampstead and Highgate, Blackheath and Strand-on-the-Green are not the only London 'villages'. There are hundreds more places much less pretty but with not only a strong sense of community, but a strong visual personality. They are different. We may not always find their character beautiful, but they are distinctive, recognizable as being themselves and not just another mid-twentieth century

Hackney Council labelled these houses at Mapledene 'unfit' and incapable of worthwhile improvement. The Minister and his inspector disagreed. The area is now being rehabilitated

shopping parade, or council or spec developer's estate. Here, as much as with historic towns or listed buildings, the dictum of that admirable conservation architect, Donald Insall, should be pinned on every architect's and planning officer's wall: 'We should try,' he says, 'to make every place of any character "daily more itself".'[8] So let us treat fashions in materials and styles with caution, and substitute instead an attitude of architectural *vive la différence*.

1. Rasmussen, S. E., *London, the Unique City*, Cape, 1973; republished Pelican, 1960
2. Taylor, Nicholas, *The Village in the City*, Temple Smith, 1973
3. Town and Country Amenities Act, 1974
4. R.I.B.A. Conference, Durham, 1974 (final day)
5. It was 'the Jago' of Arthur Morrison's novel *A Child of the Jago*, republished Panther, 1971
6. Quoted in *The Architects' Journal*, 1 August 1973
7. *The Architects' Journal*, 10 May 1972, and 1 August 1973
8. At annual conference of the Council for the Protection of Rural England, Colchester, 1971

8 THE DESTRUCTION OF THE COUNTRYSIDE

CHANGE in Britain's countryside, like change in its towns, has two facets that threaten. Destruction of the physical fabric is the more obvious one. The other is destruction of people's psychological and spiritual, their aesthetic – even artistic – heritage. We must be careful, here especially, to try to distinguish between fact and emotion. We must do so not because the emotional aspect is unimportant – far from it! – but because confusing the two allows the proponents of harmful change to argue that the case for limiting change is based wholly or largely on emotion. (Opponents of change, in the countryside as elsewhere, often make the mistake of attributing only the worst motives to the other side. Though sometimes the motive is indeed simply profit, pursued regardless of the damage it causes, it is as well to remember that most promoters of change regard what they are doing as on balance beneficial, or at least genuinely regard the damage done as a reasonable price for 'progress'. As indeed it may be in many cases.)

In separating fact from emotion, we should perhaps start by making the point that much of our landscape, especially in England – less so in Wales or Scotland – is man-made. It is often the product of centuries of conscious and deliberate change. Men cleared forests, drained marshland, planted crops and trees as wind-breaks or for the adornment of the landscape. They built roads and tramped footpaths. Even a so-called 'Area of Outstanding *Natural* Beauty' (my italics) may be artificial in this sense. Such change has generally, but by no means always, been utilitarian. It has also for the most part been relatively gradual.

But there is also landscape in which conscious visual artifice played a part. The change was brought about not by a Coke of Norfolk primarily in the interests of more efficient agriculture, but by a Capability Brown or a Humphry Repton in the process of creating a piece of landscape architecture. The English tradition for which they and their contemporaries were responsible was one of natural-seeming parkland. It is, however, an illusion of nature created by conscious artifice. It is artificial in a more thorough-going sense than land cleared and planted for agriculture.

Finally, at the other extreme, we have Britain's truly 'wild' places: areas of mountain and moorland, marsh and (in a few places) forest which are what they are without man's intervention. The biggest man-made change is probably the path or track you follow if you visit them. Change in the postwar decades, altering what is familiar and loved in our countryside, may be change from any one of these three starting points.

Following pages. Left: A traditional hedge, expertly 'laid' which is cheaper to maintain. Right: a wire fence, Bottom: The new landscape of economic agriculture – Salisbury Plain

It may be change of a variety of kinds: visual, ecological, economic or social. It may be brought about deliberately by man, or be the accidental by-product of a deliberate course of action. It may result from an accident of nature only incidentally aided, or not aided at all, by man's intervention. For example, the demands of mechanized agriculture for larger fields have altered the appearance of huge areas of English countryside. They have also, by destroying the hedgerow habitat of countless birds, small mammals, insects and plants, damaged or severed innumerable natural life-support chains and thus impoverished our wildlife heritage.[1]

It is all so much more complex than man once supposed. Farmers and foresters, taking what appear to them simple actions to protect their crops, set off undreamed-of chain reactions which may have dire consequences elsewhere. Sometimes their 'simple actions' even prove on closer examination to be counter-productive. The B.B.C.'s excellent *The World About Us* series, in a programme on the woodpecker, told how generations of foresters had regarded the bird as a threat to trees. They had seen its sharp bill attacking the timber. But careful research and examination of the evidence showed the reverse to be true. The woodpecker in question feeds on wood-boring insects. Its absence, not its presence, is a threat to the forester's crop. We know not what we do.

The farmer who destroys hedgerows because he wants larger fields for the more efficient use of his tractors and farm machines can scarcely be blamed. He is responding to short-term economic pressures, striving to answer the demand for cheap food. Much the same can be said of our National Grid of electricity transmission lines. It is man (in the shape of the Central Electricity Generating Board) responding to a strong and specific demand for cheaper power. The public sense that the British landscape should be preserved is in general a weaker and more diffuse force. Electricity suppliers, unlike farmers, have a statutory duty to 'have regard to' amenity considerations. But this is a vague and generalized duty. The statutory obligation laid on the electricity industry to balance its book is both stronger and more precise.

Many people, seeing a familiar and beautiful landscape damaged and altered by a giant line of 190ft-high pylons, ask: 'Why not put it underground? After all, they do in towns.' The generating board's reason for not normally doing so has, until recently, appeared unanswerable. It is that high voltage supplies of alternating current generates large amounts of heat.

Overhead transmission allows this to disperse. When cables are placed underground, even for short distances, elaborate and expensive measures have to be taken to cool them. For instance, where the London ring of transmission lines crosses the Thames near Tilbury, it runs through a tunnel, built for the purpose, in which the cables run in and out of troughs of water. The cost of undergrounding Supergrid supplies of alternating current is, per mile, much the same as the cost of building a six-lane motorway. It is nine or ten times as much as overhead lines, and therefore can be afforded only for relatively short stretches, such as to safeguard a nationally renowned vista in a National Park.

That was always the argument. Research into ways of cutting the cost of undergrounding a.c. cables produced no miracle solutions. But the key to the problem may lie in the words 'alternating current'. A conference organized by the Institution of Electrical Engineers in 1973 showed increasing interest in direct current methods of transmission. Mr G. C. Gracey, a civil engineer, has pointed out[2] the possible implications of this for the British landscape. First, direct current generates less heat; therefore cables can be laid underground more cheaply and easily in areas of landscape importance. Second, overhead lines can be carried on lower and less bulky pylons. Mr Gracey, it should be added, saw this more as a means to limiting the increase in numbers and size of pylons to carry higher and higher voltages than as a means of getting rid of the overhead lines we already have.

We have earlier noticed that change in the countryside has generally been, until the last two decades or so, a gradual process. In a sense, it had to be. The means were usually not to hand for more sudden and drastic changes. Today's mechanical and chemical instruments of change have altered that. But they have not greatly altered the time-scale of growth. Urban man, who sees his surroundings transformed – and the change completed – in a matter of months, does not always appreciate the rural time-scale. He has been made forcibly aware of it by the epidemic of Dutch elm disease which ravaged Britain's woods and hedgerows during the early 1970s. The apparently uncontrollable spread of the disease denuded many stretches of landscape of their finest (and sometimes only) vertical features, and left them looking more naked than they had for centuries.[3] And as the disease raged, argument raged too, among foresters, landscape architects and others. Could earlier, firmer government action have halted the disease's spread? Expensive injections for key trees were neither certain in their effect nor, clearly, a general remedy. Felling and burning of infected bark

Dutch elm disease.
Left: A healthy tree;
right: an infected
tree; centre: a dead
tree

needed to be carried out reliably, early, and in every case of infection, if they were to work. Ignorance and expense militated against this. In some sense it is almost certain that the toll from Dutch elm disease results from human interference with nature, either in transmitting the disease to places where no natural forces exist to counteract it or in destroying the mechanisms that would have held it in check. It is idle to regret the nature of our 1970s world. But the Dutch elm disease epidemic does make us aware how vulnerable some supposedly permanent features of our landscape are, and how long they take to replace. For all our talk of instant landscape, and use of semi-mature silver birches in concrete tubs to brighten urban wastelands, we have as yet found no way to grow an elm to maturity in months. So the view from the window that a man or woman of fifty may have known all his life can vanish. There is no replacement in his lifetime. Left to themselves, the eco-systems might (at some cost) have coped. We, with our imperfect and tardy procedures for tree-felling orders and our arguments about grants and enforcement – we did not and could not cope. It will take not only money and effort to repair, but time. And time is the rural dimension that urban Britain least understands.

New farming methods apart, the three activities which have probably made the biggest impact on the countryside are road

building, housing development, and mining and quarrying. Roads are discussed in Chapter 12; housing in chapter 10. Quarrying we shall look at here. And we must start by recognizing an unfortunate geological fact: many of our wildest and most beautiful areas, often in theory protected by National Park status, are precisely those richest in much-sought-after and easily extracted minerals. Thus, the North Yorks National Park has rich deposits of potash, and potash mining has been sanctioned at three different sites.[4] Only one of them is so far active. That, however, is a result more of the state of world markets than of any tenderness on the part of mining companies towards outstanding natural beauty.

Another National Park, the Peak District, is the source of much of its region's limestone supply. This fact of geology explains the curious shape of the National Park boundary, with its long neck of countryside excluded from the designated area running fifteen miles into the park and taking New Mills, Whaley Bridge and even Buxton out of the protected area. These areas were, it was argued, already industrialized. Even so, limestone quarrying does go on within the park and has, in some people's view, ruined a number of valleys, notably Middletondale. Limestone production in the Peak District (inside and outside the National Park) rose from 770,000 tons in 1951 to 2·25 million tons in 1961. By 1971 it had reached more than 19m. tons. The official guide to the Peak District National Park pinpoints the problem. 'Limestone is used in the manufacture of chemicals, in steel making (as a flux), for cement, for roadstone and of course the original use, in farming, to improve acid land. All the first three uses need stone which is chemically very pure. The purest limestone happens to lie in a ring around the great dome of the limestone country, and this is where most of the quarries are.'[5]

Limestone quarried in the actual National Park goes mostly for road buildings. And though fewer men work in the quarries, mechanization has greatly increased their ability to cut great holes in the landscape. The same National Park Guide already cited says mutedly: 'It is rather a problem to keep the industry going without eating up too much of the country. A big limestone quarry can be impressive, but the vertical steel kilns in which the stone is burnt for lime are ugly, and so is the black smoke they emit.'[6] Cement production within and close to the edge of the park requires shale as well as limestone, and digging shale leaves large and ugly gashes in the landscape. Even in favourable circumstances, with careful control and relatively generous allocation of funds for landscaping and reinstatement, the wounds take a long time to heal. And even when they do, a sense of wilderness may have been lost for ever. One of the main burdens of the Peak Park board's final report before its reconstitution in April 1974 at the time of local government reorganization had to do with mineral extraction. A major lesson of twenty-two years as a planning authority was: 'We need more detailed and effective control over mineral extraction if this industry is not to go on unnecessarily making a mess in our National Park.'

The Snowdonia National Park has long provided slate in large quantities, and again some of the oddities of the National Park boundary can be attributed to the presence of this long-standing industry. More recently a combination of high world prices and modern mining technology made it worthwhile for Rio Tinto Zinc to seek permission to cut away at the hillside of Coed y Brenin, an attractive and little-populated area of hills, forests and rushing streams north of Dolgelly. At the same time they sought permission to dredge the beautiful Mawddach estuary for gold. High metal prices and new machinery for dredging and sifting made it for the first time both feasible and apparently profitable for them to contemplate this. There was great opposition, especially to the estuarial dredging, and this latter proposal was dropped. The way in which Rio Tinto's chairman casually conceded this point in a television documentary on Snowdonia in 1972 suggested to some suspicious minds that gold was either a bargaining counter which the firm had always been prepared to drop, or that the economics of the operation had changed again.

At Coed y Brenin, Rio Tinto began drilling without planning permission. The planning authority belatedly took them to task for this, rejecting the firm's argument that drilling did not constitute a development for which consent was needed. It does. A subsequent public enquiry gave permission, and other firms began prospecting on locations elsewhere in Snowdonia, also buying options from farmers on land thought to have a commercially exploitable mineral content. Rio Tinto later stated that they were not proceeding with exploration, because copper was not present in commercial quantities. It should, however, be noted that the test of what is commercial varies with world markets. By August 1974, this particular threat to Snowdonia appeared to have receded; but it had demonstrated how inadequate local planning control was in the early 1970s to deal with it. A large international mining company could run circles round the planning authorities. Maybe the larger, reorganized Welsh counties could now do better. I suspect that national park conservation policies would still look rather fragile against pressures for exploiting 'home-grown' mineral resources.

National Parks are not the only places drastically affected by mineral extraction. Those who blandly assumed that change in the countryside is more gradual and less drastic than in towns and city should look at mining in Somerset's Mendip Hills. Anyone who grew up there in the 1940s and then, say, emigrated to Australia, and returned only in 1975, might very well lose himself completely trying to walk on parts of Mendip that are simply no longer there. Dulcote Hill, between Wells and Shepton Mallet, is 20–50ft lower than it was in 1945. The pleasant walk along its top, craggy and turfed in a typical Mendip way, has gone. It fell a victim to large-scale, mechanized quarrying. Dr William Stanton, an authority on Mendip whose voice is listened to with respect by the quarrying companies as well as by the preservationists, calculates that, of the 60 million tons of available limestone in Dulcote Hill, 15 million tons – a quarter – has been taken.

The Hermon Valley, Coed-y-Brenin, in Snowdonia. Here Rio Tinto Zinc bored for copper

From the point of view of landscape, Sandford Hill in western Mendip has been, and is being, even more drastically affected. Again the craggy, turfy top has gone. The hill is being quarried out like a hollow tooth. An existing planning permission allows the quarrying company to enlarge the width of the quarry entrance to 500 metres – wider than the world's tallest building is high. This great gap will be punched in the westerly bastion of Mendip on the side where it is most visible from the flat Somerset plain to the west. The arguments for and against quarrying on Mendip and elsewhere on this scale are tied up with the debates about 'limits of growth' and prodigal use of non-renewable resources as much as with conflicts between material progress and conservation of our non-material treasures. The conser-

Modern quarrying is on a different scale from the old. Batts Coombe Quarry, Cheddar

vationists on Mendip are fighting not just for the view from
their own back windows, or freedom from lanes made dusty
and dangerous by gravel lorries, or respite from things that go
bump in the middle of a tranquil Somerset afternoon. They are
fighting passionately also for the last stretch of wild land,
mysterious and untouched even by agricultural improvers,
within easy range of the Bristol conurbation. It is, they say, our
spiritual as well as our ecological heritage that is at stake. But
to many people, that sounds a flimsy, metaphysical argument
when weighed against the case for quarrying, which runs something like this: 'You comfortably-off middle-class professionals
living in stone cottages on Mendip and often commuting to
Bristol or Bath, have your cars and your comfort. Millions do
not. They lack good schools and hospitals and aspire to escape
depressing urban environments by owning and using cars.
Cars need roads; roads, schools, hospitals, all demand cement
and aggregates. You, who have all these, would deny them to
others. And you would deny jobs to the local people.'

That, at least, has traditionally been the argument. It may be
bending a little now with the growing consciousness that we
cannot be too profligate with either energy or finite raw
materials. The Mendip conservationists tend to say (a) our
society must moderate its demands for scarce raw materials and
(b) it should take them first from other less precious areas like
south Gloucestershire. But unfortunately economics dictate
otherwise. Transport is a major ingredient in the delivered price
of aggregates and every mile adds significantly to the cost.
Without some environmental tax which bears most heavily on
extraction in designated National Parks and areas of outstanding
natural beauty, this is unlikely to impress the quarrying companies. Meanwhile, above Cheddar and close to its famous
gorge, Batts Coombe Quarry is a gash 500 yards wide and
growing. 'Quarry' no longer means a little hole in the hillside
where the local builder or the local council take as they need
them small supplies of stone and gravel for local needs. 'Quarry'
means big business, mechanized and with all the disturbance of
transport by (at best) railway and (at worst) scores of heavy
mineral lorries on narrow country lanes. In 1947 the total
limestone quarried in Somerset was 1·2 million tons. By 1972
it was 12 million tons. In 1947 all the centuries of small quarrying
that had taken place on Mendip had 'worked and won' no more
than 50 million tons. A quarter of a century later, in 1972, that
cumulative total was 100 million tons. Man had quarried as
much in twenty-five years as in the previous twenty-five
centuries.

Forestry is another form of 'development' which has steadily changed the face of the British countryside. The change is of two main kinds: (1) woodlands that have traditionally been deciduous or hardwoods are replanted with conifers (softwoods) because that is the more profitable and quicker-growing crop; and (2) planting of areas that have in the past been open land, such as the uplands of central Wales which were either wild moorland or pasture for a kind of sheep farming that has become less and less economic. Opposition to conifer afforestation derives from two inter-connected reactions. Conservationists dislike the transformation of the landscape it produces. The forests mask the contours of the hills and reduce the variety of colouring and texture, they say. And active walkers and climbers find their routes blocked by thick planting and, where paths are usable, find the going much duller because, instead of the variety of view enjoyed from a path through open uplands, they are for too much of the route walking between walls of trees.

A survey carried out by a volunteer group from the Youth Hostels Association in mid-Wales in 1972 and published in the summer of 1974, illustrates these changes and reactions to them very clearly.[7] The group looked at (that is to say, on the ground by walking or cycling) some 250 square miles in southern mid-Wales which had been the subject of a previous survey nine years before. Surveying the area in 1 km grid squares, they found that forestry had increased by about 50 per cent, and that the predominant species were sitka spruce followed by larch and pine. They found that 'perhaps the most notable effect of the introduction of commercial forest on most of the land surveyed was the reduction in variety of colour and form. This was particularly the case in valleys, where sheep country is richly varied in these respects; in general, *the poorer the pasture, the greater the variety found*.'[8] I italicize the last phrase because it seems to underline the recurrent conflict between wild beauty and economics. They continue: 'On much of the high land, forests have little effect on form and can, with species mixing, produce greater colour variety than the pasture had. It is worth noting, however, that the overall "tone" of forest is nearly always darker than pasture. This was vividly illustrated by surveyors who observed that cloud shadows could easily be mistaken for forest at a distance.'[9] After commenting on blocking or restriction of long views, the report adds: 'Even at close quarters, rivers and streams and rock outcrop which in sheep country are distinctive features are obscured by close planting.'[10]

The Y.H.A. survey (whose authors are careful not to claim too much for what, they stress, was an amateur undertaking) is

Ramblers object to the spread of conifers, which screen long views and make for duller walking

revealing both as a close-up objective look at the effects of commercial forestry on fine walking country, and for the subjective reactions it records from a group of hill walkers to a landscape transformed by afforestation. It should be noted that a high proportion of the 'surveyors' had either not seen it before or did not know it in its previous state. They were asked to say in respect of each 1 km square with little or no forest whether afforestation would depreciate, or might improve the landscape, or whether its effect would be neutral. Where substantial forest already existed, they were asked whether the landscape was in their view the poorer, or whether they liked the planted areas, or found them acceptable but thought more would depreciate the landscape, or thought the effect neutral. In the areas with little or no existing forest, 80 per cent of the grid squares evoked the response 'Afforestation would depreciate the landscape'; in 8 per cent the surveyors thought it might improve it; and in 12 per cent the response was neutral. In existing forest areas, 58·5 per cent of grid squares were thought to be the poorer in landscape terms either actually or potentially after trees had grown taller; in 21 per cent the result was neutral; in 9 per cent acceptable but damaging if carried any further; and in 11·5 per cent the surveyors liked the effect of planting.

Now the authors of the report do not make any special claim that these views are representative of youth hostellers or hill walkers, let alone the general public. It does, however, underline a frequently-expressed conservationist/recreational lobby view on afforestation and, in the survey area, the drastic nature and impact of the change. Yet forestry, even on the largest scale, is one of those activities not covered by planning control. The anomalous nature of this gap in planning law will be appreciated when we observe that, to extend or rebuild a small stone cottage in such an area, you will almost certainly be subject to stringent planning control. But you can, by afforestation, change the nature and look of miles of hillside and, at most (even if you are the Forestry Commission), your only duty will be to 'consult' the planning authority.

The need for forestry to be brought under planning control, long urged by the amenity/recreational lobby and by official bodies such as county councils and National Park authorities, was officially endorsed in 1973. A committee set up by the government under the chairmanship of a then D.O.E. minister, Lord Sandford, to review the status and future of the National Parks, urged[11] in these areas it should indeed require planning consent. But in July 1974 a new government chose to ignore this recommendation and announced new 'consultative procedures' which would be binding on the Forestry Commission, the largest developer by afforestation. This is unlikely to be an adequate substitute for statutory control. Writing to Mr Denis Howell, who had been appointed Minister of State for Sport and Recreation, the national secretary of the Ramblers' Association, Alan Mattingly, voiced the disappointment of his organization at this decision and explained why his members were so concerned about afforestation. It eroded, he said,[12] 'That most basic of recreational resources – fine open moorland country. Hill walking,' he went on, 'is one of the most popular recreations; and this popularity is growing as fast as that of any other major recreation. Yet the spread of conifer plantations is reducing the areas sought out by the hill walker at an alarming rate – nearly 100,000 acres per annum according to the Forestry Commission's annual report.'

The Ramblers and the conservation lobby were the more angered by the government's decision (announced, significantly, by the Ministry of Agriculture, a 'developing' department, rather than by the D.O.E., the 'controlling' one) because of what they saw as the nature of commercial forestry. Mr Mattingly, speaking at an association meeting in Norwich, attacked the 'scandalous tax concessions available to owners of private forests'[13] and quoted *The Economist*[14] in support of this view. The real attraction of forestry was 'the tax games that can be played with it: no capital gains tax and a choice between Schedule B, where a nominal flat rate of tax is paid when the trees are felled, and Schedule D, where ordinary tax is paid on timber sold, but the costs of maintenance and re-planting are set against other income. An owner,' continued *The Economist* article, 'can move from B to D as it suits him.' By contrast, complained Mattingly, the hill farmer, who was often displaced by the forester, has no such advantage. His contribution to the balance of payments was no less important. Moreover the nature of his work served to safeguard the beauty of the uplands.

As the Y.H.A. mid-Wales report cited above made clear, the Forestry Commission's practice has in some respects improved. Under pressure from amenity interests, they now temper the sharp edges of their commercial forests with mixed planting and make some 'amenity provision'. But this too often consists of a car-park-cum-picnic-site with perhaps a nature trail, but without much regard to the needs of the serious walker or the country lover who wants to see the shape of the uplands or savour unfolding long views as he follows his path.

1. The Council for the Protection of Rural England estimates that Britain's 600,000 miles of surviving hedgerows, on average 2 yards wide, provide 400,000 acres of good habitat for animal and plant life – twice the total area of national nature reserves. Destruction of hedgerows has seriously depleted numbers of blackbirds and 44 other varieties of birds and threatened 250 varieties of flowering plant. The C.P.R.E. estimates that a mile of hedgerow contains on average 22 wild birds, an equivalent area of open country only about 6 birds.
2. *Bulletin*, Council for the Protection of Rural England, April/May 1974
3. Dutch elm disease is estimated to have killed 20 per cent of the elms in southern England (*Observer Magazine*, 19 May 1974)
4. For an account of these potash mining projects see Aldous, T., *Battle for the Environment*, Fontana, 1972, pp. 216–220
5. *Peak District: National Park Guide No. 3*, H.M.S.O., 1971, p. 49
6. Ibid
7, 8, 9, 10. *Landscape and Forestry in Mid-Wales: a land-use survey*, Youth Hostels Association National Countryside Committee, August 1974
11. *National Park Review Police Committee report*, H.M.S.O., 1974
12. Letter from Mattingley to Howell dated 18 July 1974
13. Mattingley: speech at Norwich, 13 July 1974
14. *The Economist*, 22 June 1974, quoted by Mattingley in above speech

9 THE INVADERS: HOUSES & PEOPLE

CREEPING urbanization is another major threat, in the form chiefly of housing and industry. The Council for the Protection of Rural England has calculated that Britain loses some 50,000 acres a year of its countryside to development of this kind. And in its report *Urban Pressures on the Countryside*[1] the Committee for Environmental Conservation (CoEnCo), which is a co-ordinating body for a whole range of organizations concerned with the countryside, estimated that 500,000 rural acres had been urbanized in the decade to 1972, and that another 1·5 million acres would be urbanized by the year 2,000. But these overall figures were guess estimates. CoEnCo conceded that Britain lacked firm and detailed statistics about changes of land use. This is still to a large extent so. But Dr Robin Best of the Department of Countryside Planning at London University's Wye College in Kent has been able to clarify the situation for me a good deal. Though urbanization of rural acres continues at an alarming rate, it is, he points out, not as great in quantitative terms as in the 1930s. Then, to a great extent as a result of suburban growth round London and other large cities, some 60,000 acres were being lost to agriculture in England and Wales. In the postwar period 1945–70 the average rate per year has been about 38,000 acres, and in the 1960s – thought of by many people as the period of rampant urbanization – it averaged only little more than 40,000 acres a year.[2] No precise statistics exist as to how much of this land was lost to housing and how much to industry. Modern industrial complexes like the petro-chemicals of Teeside and Grangemouth look – and indeed are – vast, but they represent concentration, and so in a sense economy of land use. The average annual loss of agricultural land to urban development in England, Wales and Scotland during the 1960s – around 47,000 acres – is significantly less than that lost to forestry – about 62,500 acres. But, of course, these statistics speak only of acreages. Giant cooling towers for power stations, the flares of oil refineries, or the tall chimneys of cement works and potash mines may have an effect on the landscape out of all proportion to the size of sites they occupy.

One at first sight puzzling feature of these statistics when broken down by region is that the biggest losses of agricultural land in the postwar period have been occurring not, as one might expect, in the London and southeastern region, but in Cheshire, Lancashire and Durham – all counties where population has been almost static. In the five years 1962–67, these counties lost 0·3 per cent of their total areas to urban development; the London region only a third of that proportion. The reason

seems to be that many towns in these counties have been experiencing a comparable spread of suburban development as London had in the 1930s (though under tighter planning control). Their new towns are also in the growth stage: London's inner ring of 1940s and 1950s new towns has largely stopped growing. Development in the London region is now tending more and more to be by infill of what were fairly low density suburbs; incursions into the green belt are only exceptionally sanctioned. It is big suburban gardens that are taking most metropolitan growth, not its surrounding green acres.

The eating up of acres is one aspect of urbanization; the manner of doing so is another. We have been better at keeping the 'quaint' set-pieces of village green, inn and church than at preserving the overall visual character of the village. In the prodigal postwar decades when town centres and urban neighbourhoods were torn down and rebuilt bigger but not better, country people also had their go at destruction. Houses and cottages which were important to the overall scene and which could have been turned into decent homes with today's outlay of effort, ingenuity and improvement grants, were torn down or allowed to fall derelict whilst at the edges of the village new (and usually alien) development took place. Rows of council houses decent enough in their functional provision, but generally places apart both in siting and in their unmistakeably 'council' style; and 'spec' estates of gimmicky, subtopian semis or bungalows in styles and materials that had even less to do with the local vernacular – these two kinds of development blew many villages apart visually and, sometimes, socially. I have heard a skilful and sensitive architect tell, with grim humour, of submitting plans for rural council housing to an R.D.C. housing committee. Having managed to produce homes both up to the required Parker Morris standards of space and provision of built-in facilities and keeping within the government cost yardstick ceiling, and on top of that to produce something that fitted into the scale and style of the village concerned, he arrived at the meeting feeling rather pleased with himself. The councillors who were his client soon altered that. 'But they don't look like council houses,' they exclaimed. The tone was not one of congratulation, they were complaining at a shocking breach of the municipal decencies.

Sometimes the spoliation of a village is largely or entirely of internal generation. Rural communities are often a decade or more behind the prevailing fashions, and this has been to some extent true of their adoption of the trend from uncritical redevelopment to selective conservation and unfill. A Welsh farmer and his wife we once stayed with (real working dairy farmers, Welsh-speaking and supporters of Plaid Cymru into the bargain) lived in an old stone manse furnished in 'natural' good taste with Welsh dresser type furniture and rugs and polished floors. But, we discovered, they were just waiting for the day they retired, when they could hand the farmhouse over to the children, and move to a new house of what looked like grey concrete blocks at the end of the farm drive. That was not in a village. But the 'grey concrete block' mentality, or the assumption that what is new and shiny is best and country people deserve it, has ruined many attractive villages. It has certainly made many unsensational but inoffensive ones seriously offend our sense of what is in place.

In other places, development from outside, or the pressures of commuters or immigration from the towns, has caused the damage. Peter Ambrose, in his thoughtful and perceptive *Quiet Revolution: Social Change in a Sussex Village, 1871–1971*,[3] makes this point well. His village is Ringmer in Sussex. Socially it is a healthier and more variegated village now than a century ago. Some of the prime failings of the postwar decades, he argues, are in planning and housing. Most of the new building in Ringmer has been aesthetically dismal, he says, and is perceived by the villagers to be so. But over and above that, the effects of land ownership and developers' *modus operandi* (municipal as well as private) has been to separate out different social groups into different places and different existences: not just rich from poor, but car-owning from non-car-owning and one-car family from two-car family. Some of the separation is due to the accident of cheap land in an out-of-the-way location where the local council built an estate. Some results from growth of traffic. But the out-of-character design of much of the new housing certainly reinforces people's consciousness of it. When Ambrose did a social survey of his fellow villagers, the answers to his questions on this subject could almost be summed up as: Development, all right, but why did it have to be so ugly and out-of-place? Of one new private housing development, one respondent told him: '[It] is an *urban* development, bleak, cold and out of character with the village.' Another said: '[It] is very bad, no thought has been given to retaining the village character, and all the other estates are bad. I am not saying expansion in itself is bad, only the character of the present development.' Another: 'They keep building suburban type, uninteresting houses, all similar, instead of retaining the village atmosphere with carefully planned buildings.' And another: 'Architecturally the new buildings are appalling; either very ugly with no personality or

character, or else pseudo-regency, which just isn't in place here at all.'[4]

Perhaps part of the trouble is not (as some of Dr Ambrose's respondents declared) that there was 'no planning', but that protective planning for villages for most of the postwar period was half-hearted and, above all, negative. No one told the small developer or builder what to do or how to do it. Only in the last few years have clear policy statements arrived for conservation areas; and advisory booklets like the C.P.R.E.'s *The Future of the Village* been followed (this only in 1973) by the kind of positive planning contained in Essex County Council's *Design Guide for Residential Areas*.[5] Creative planning for a village requires an intimate acquaintance with the place on the ground, how it works and what makes it tick, as well as a sound understanding of the building styles, methods and materials that have made it what it is. And this must be built on with skilful diplomacy, persuasion and compromise between ideal solutions and what is economic. It is all much more difficult and demanding than simply reacting negatively to what the developer proposes. But once it begins to stick, the effect in terms of environmental education can snowball.

Country (as distinct from town) planning, as the CoEnCo Pressures report lamented, and as Britain's one Professor of Countryside Planning continually complains,[6] has too long been the Cinderella of our planning system. Mineral extraction is too loosely controlled; farm buildings are for the most part not controlled at all; forestry is not controlled; and the standard of development control for many villages has, to judge by the results, been woefully inadequate. But though much damage has been done, there is still much in the British countryside worth saving. And as the scale and pace of development increases, it becomes the more imperative not only to have more comprehensive countryside planning, but to use it more effectively and positively.

This applies above all to recreational planning and management – the two terms overlap, and the best practitioners tend to operate at both levels. It is a relatively new activity in Britain, and still comes low on most planning authorities' lists of priorities. But its importance and, indeed, acute urgency, are now increasingly being recognized. Thus, when the Royal Town Planning Institute elected their first woman president, Sylvia Law, in July 1974, they were also choosing as the profession's chief spokesman a rather different kind of planner from those who had represented them in the past: not an architect turned local authority planner, but someone whose job it was, at the

Tarn Hows in the Lake District. Visitors' cars and feet threatened to erode its fragile beauty. The National Trust had to divert these pressures

G.L.C., to find out people's recreational habits and needs and plan to cater for them. One of the difficulties in doing so, she says, is that recreational movement, unlike journey-to-work travel, is a capricious quantity. Survey work at the G.L.C. has disposed of the myth that London 'empties' into the countryside at weekends. In fact, only about 4 per cent of Londoners travel into the countryside. 'But that 4 per cent is 300,000,' she points out, 'which is enough to put a fairly hefty strain on roads and transport. Even a 1 per cent change can make a startling difference.'[7]

If it makes a startling difference to the means of transport, the impact on a suddenly popular destination can be even more dramatic. Even if all visitors to the countryside respected the Country Code, which they do not, sheer exposure to people's feet can be extremely damaging. Instances of this have been reported in recent years at Box Hill in Surrey, on parts of the Pennine Way, and in the Lake District. At one National Trust property in the Lake District, Tarn Hows, erosion reached alarming proportions. A traffic count showed that in 1972 149,000 cars containing about 550,000 people visited this

sensitive, even vulnerable little beauty spot of whom 55,000 walked right round the Tarn. The effect of so many visitors walking over a comparatively small area was to wear away footpaths and denude surrounding sections of hillside of grass. The beauty spot was well on the way to becoming a dust-bowl or, in wet weather, a mudbath. The trust had to act firmly if Tarn Hows' own popularity was not to ruin it. They fenced off one of the more sensitive areas of hillside to allow it to be repaired and recover, and also closed one car park to all save the disabled.

But, as the National Trust realized only too well, saying No is not enough. People spilling into the countryside in large numbers, whether by car or (when they get there) on foot, are a destructive force unless offered something to do when they arrive. The idea that, when faced with the natural world, people

Below: Fell Foot country park, Windermere. A National Trust 'honey pot' on the edge of the lake draws away what might otherwise be the destructive pressure of car-borne visitors to the southern Lake District

Right: A new footbridge at Newtown, Montgomeryshire. Modern structures can be elegant, economical and in keeping with their surroundings

should and can be left to commune with it without the offer of information and guidance is just not tenable in an age of mass, motorized recreation. So at Tarn Hows itself, while shutting off certain areas and restricting car parking (principally to a car park hidden in a dell among trees), the Trust also attempted to provide positive answers. One of them was a clearly sign-posted nature walk, for instance. This kind of discreet attraction to pull people away from where they will do damage is a very local application of the 'honeypot' principle. This can also operate at a different scale to draw people away from vulnerable areas much earlier in their recreation-seeking trip. Thus in the Lakes, the National Trust has created a major 'honeypot' at Fell Foot at the southern end of Windermere. Trust officials were all too conscious that there are very few places where the public have access to the waterside on the eastern shore of

Windermere. Families come to 'the Lakes' and are frustrated because they cannot get at them. Fell Foot is the site and park of a demolished mansion, given to the Trust in 1948 to do what they thought best with it. And what they have now done with it is very constructive in a number of ways. As Christopher Hanson-Smith of the Trust's North-West (or Lakeland) Region puts it: 'It is somewhere where you can get to the lake with your car, and children can paddle and fool around without any conflict with farmers or sheep.' The main car park is well hidden in a dip, as is a caravan park. A score of cedar-clad holiday bungalows, let by the week, are dotted among the trees on rising ground, and there are a café and visitor centre close to the

147

lake, where boats are for hire. There is some argument in conservationist circles about such 'honeypots'. If the honey is too sticky, will it not pull more bees towards the beauty spots? The answer must be that the attractive force is in the appeal of the area itself – the Lake District, in this case – and that people will come. If you do not cater for and guide them, you court frustration, lack of appreciation, and ultimately destruction of one kind or another – if in no other way, from the pressure of motor traffic trying to penetrate areas where, environmentally speaking, there is no room for it. The concept of the 'environmental capacity' of urban streets introduced by the Buchanan team in *Traffic in Towns* clearly has its rural counterpart. But the environmental qualities we seek to conserve in such areas as Lakeland are more fragile and the capacities much lower.

Increasingly the notion of saying 'No' to the car in rural beauty spots, but providing alternative means of visitor access, is gaining ground. The Peak Park Planning Board's minibus experiment at Goyt Valley was a notable pioneer. The Board, taking advantage of the new financial deal for National Park authorities in 1974, carried the principle behind this very much further. In this area, at least, where there is a strong tradition of hill walking and open air recreation, it was plain that large numbers of people from the urban areas that surround the national park were being forced to use the private car to get to their walks and picnic places because during the 1960s bus services had become run-down. This is a familiar situation in many other areas – in the Yorkshire Dales, for instance, a combination of Beeching's Axe and diminishing bus services meant that, by the early 1960s, a Sunday walk up the Wharf valley above Bolton Abbey could only be continued after about 3.30 p.m. either by car or by hitch-hiking back into the West Riding conurbation. The Peak Park board, with a little extra money in the kitty and clear proof of the growing numbers of visitors to certain parts of the national park, set out to remedy this. By spending a modest £2,000–£3,000 in guarantees to the bus operators, they were able to ensure bus services on summer Sundays to popular starting points for walks at something like an hourly frequency. And they took the trouble to publicize these services, which they dubbed 'Pathfinders'.[8] Of course, this did not result in all the motorists locking their cars in their garages and going by bus. But we have already seen that it is the marginal percentage increase or decrease in recreational car use that can make all the difference. And in the summer of 1974, the signs were that a significant number of car-owners were saying: 'We don't really want to be lumbered with the

Goyt Valley with cars banned. A minibus brings people in from the peripheral car parks. Contrast the scene on pp. 136–7

thing. If we can be sure of a regular bus service, then we'll go by bus and walk to somewhere else where we can pick up a bus home.' Liberation from that commitment to get back to the car at the end of a country walk can be quite exhilarating. And people who are not at the wheel when they penetrate the countryside are, it seems, more likely to appreciate its scale and tempo and fragility: less likely to assist (wittingly or unwittingly) in its destruction.

1. Coenco, 1972
2. See also Best, Robin: *Geographical Magazine*, October 1972; *New Society*, 2 April 1970
3. Ambrose, Peter, *The Quiet Revolution: Social Change in a Sussex Village, 1871–1971*, Chatto & Windus, 1974
4. Ambrose, op. cit., p. 151
5. Essex County Council, 1973
6. For instance, at the Town and Country Planning Association's conference on *Second Homes*, Birmingham, 1 May 1974
7. *The Times*, 12 July 1974
8. Two other national parks, Northumberland and the Pembrokeshire coast, have also been subsidizing walkers' bus services

N January 1974 I made a lengthy pilgrimage by sleeper and
hired car to the Bay of Nigg. I went to look at an oil rig being
built there. One had heard tales and even seen photographs
of oil-rig construction, but these pale into insignificance beside
the reality. Nigg Bay lies at the eastern, seaward end of the
Cromarty Firth, north-west of and across the water from
Cromarty town where the Firth narrows before flowing out
into the sea. By road the rig construction site is twelve miles
from the nearest town, Invergordon, which has a population of
perhaps 3,000. Inverness is getting on for fifty miles away.
Despite an aluminium smelter and a distillery which have
brought a new comfortable prosperity to the area without too
much destruction of the landscape, little towns like Dingwall
(population 4,500; county town of the former Ross and
Cromarty-shire) have a quiet, gentle pace of life which is almost
as different from Inverness as Inverness from Edinburgh. It
infects even incomers like the young community development
officer from south of the border I met there. The way and pace
of life are gentle, civilized and personal; the direct antithesis of
the rush and anonymity of the big city. Without making the
mistake of romanticizing, one can say that it is a very pleasant
life-style, with a contentment and satisfaction lacking in more
urban or urbanized places. But it is also vulnerable.

You see why as you drive north from Invergordon. Across the
firth is the narrow opening to the sea, and, quite dwarfing it, the
rig. Now that, of course, is a temporary abberation. On further
examination, it seems the least of the threats. For as I went
further north, the pace and scale of life changed. Everywhere
were construction works: roads widened, hedges torn down,
corners cut away. And all the time people in a hurry: rig
construction workers driving fast to get to work or to get away
from it. Lots of money, but too little time – the reverse, almost,
of the communities round about. As you round Nigg Bay the
turmoil increases. Cars, lorries, earth-moving equipment; the
ground for a couple of miles churned up by mechanized movement. Five or six huge sheds, as big as moderate-sized factories
and (rightly) painted a dull blue-grey, indicate at once the scale
and the urgency of rig fabrication. There is too much at stake
not to put work under cover. Round the headland lie two old
Clyde steamers where construction workers live. Their life-
style is a rough, fast one. Police have been called in to break up
fights.

This and other rig construction sites in rural areas are not
only spoiling remote and beautiful stretches of coastline (local
conservationists will believe in reinstatement when they see

it),[1] but administering a series of rude shocks to the local economy and sense of community. Social workers locally, and in the Scottish Development Department in Edinburgh, express extreme pessimism about both. They are convinced that the stability of rural life will be wrecked, the economy distorted by the attraction of skilled workers away from local needs to high-pay jobs connected with oil rig construction. And when the construction boom is over, the oil flows quietly through automated pipelines with a minimum of local labour – when the bubble suddenly deflates, what then? A long and painful period of readjustment, with a coastline and beaches still scarred by the artefacts of those men in a hurry who could not wait and did not stay to pick up the pieces. Perhaps it was inevitable, perhaps the price to be paid for (relatively) cheap fuel. But Nigg will never be the same, and nor (despite the brave attempts of local planning authorities to blunt the impact) will northern Shetland round the proposed oil port of Sullom Voe.

One part of Britain that used to be as tranquil as the Cromarty Firth, but has paid the price of having a coastline, is Pembrokeshire. The coast has attracted holiday and recreational development because of its beaches and coves and havens; industrial development because of its sheltered deep water in Milford Haven. The cultural shock has neither been as sudden nor as intense, but it has been there. In the unspoilt and gentle Gwaun Valley of Welsh north Pembrokeshire, for instance, the farming families still in a local festival celebrate the new year in our mid-January according to the pre-Gregorian calendar. This is an intensely private affair, not meant for the tourists. Indeed, you may be married to a girl from the valley and still regard it as a privilege, not a right, to be invited. But in 1974 a group of outsiders hired a bus to take them from Fishguard to the festival. They were not turned away – the valley people are too well mannered – but their presence was resented. What the changes of centuries failed to destroy, the recreational explosion of the 1970s – by no means always as benign as tourist boards would have us believe – has put in jeopardy.

Tony Roberts, sometime head warden of the Pembrokeshire National Park, has farmed in the Gwaun Valley for nine years. He resigned as head warden in protest at the ineffectiveness of conservation policies in the county. In theory planning control is tight. You cannot, for instance, buy a ruined cottage hidden among woods and restore it for habitation, whether as a week-end/holiday cottage or for all-the-year-round occupation unless it was fairly recently lived in. But you can get permission to do what has infinitely more harmful impact on the environment –

put up a small estate of grey, pebbledashed bungalows on the edge of a village, on the hillside above the sea; planning theory holds that to be 'within the village envelope' – though the kind of village pattern that suggests is one on the whole alien to that part of the country.

The spread of pebbledash, in disregard of the shape of existing settlements and defiance of the natural shape of the landscape, is one form of development. Caravan sites are another. Official policy here is to limit sites for static caravans and encourage instead a rather more permanent form of holiday dwelling: the chalet. In some ways these can be a great improvement on caravan sites. For instance, the caravan site at Nolton Cross, on the coast west of Haverfordwest, is appallingly sited, right on the skyline with no attempt to hide it below the crest of the hill or in a fold in the ground. It could scarcely be more obtrusive. Less than a mile away on the other side of Nolton Haven, a group of chalets at Folkeston Lane has been well hidden in what looks like an old quarry. They replace a caravan park which was closed down. The buildings, in brick faced with rough stone, fit in reasonably well given obviously tight cost limits. The buildings also have more of a sense of permanence and belonging than the usually brightly coloured static caravan, but are scarcely suitable for all-the-year-round family occupation. The planning consent in fact stipulates that they should not be used in that way. But when I was there in March 1974, there were signs of something suspiciously like all-the-year-round occupation in one or two of them. Such planning conditions take vigilance and determination to enforce.

That aspect must also be seen against the new housing climate in the area. The second homes invasion has hit with a vengeance at least the parts of Pembrokeshire reasonably near the coast. Tony Roberts observes that in the last five years the price of smallholdings has increased tenfold. For local people they are now prohibitive. 'They're not enormous compared with a semi-detached in Woking, but they are enormous here,' he says. It has become virtually impossible for young people from the villages to buy a small-holding, or even a home of their own, in many parts of the county.[2] While the cottages their parents often strove to get out of are lovingly and lavishly converted and furnished by £15,000-a-year men from London and the Midlands, they are thrust into council houses on the edges of towns and villages, in locations that are awkward and which often produce the most damage to the landscape. Not always. Sometimes they are right in the villages. Dinas, on the north coast, is a case in point. With an incredible lack of feeling for the shape and nature of the village, the local council has built some ugly unmistakeably council houses slap up against the church.

Housing and caravans are bad enough, but compared with some of the industrial development they pale into insignificance. Gulf's Waterston oil refinery on the north shore of Milford Haven is perhaps the worst example. It is not so much the complex's intrinsic ugliness and scale that offend as its siting. It towers over the little village of Waterston, whose inhabitants have to bear its smells and dirt as well as visual spoliation of their surroundings. Yet, as is the nature of such high-technology, low employment complexes, the local community has gained very little from the vast capital input. As at Nigg, money comes in but most of it goes out again. Whatever the pros and cons of national interest, environmentally, the siting of the Gulf refinery where it is was a disastrous decision. If that was really the only feasible location, the planning authority should have demanded that the company pay for complete relocation of Waterston village and all its inhabitants. Environmentally acceptable large-scale development rarely comes on the cheap.

Pembrokeshire and Nigg illustrate some of the pressures to which Britain's coastlines have been subject in the postwar years. As to the overall picture, the National Trust estimated in 1964 that, of about 3,000 miles of British coastline, roughly 1,000 were already developed or committed to development, another 1,000 miles were of only moderate scenic beauty or recreational potential, and about 970 miles were of great scenic or recreational quality and ought to be preserved. In 1971 the Countryside Commission, official guardian of national parks and countryside amenity generally, proposed the designation of a very similar set of coastlines as 'Heritage Coasts'. It wanted them to be given statutory protection against development. The government declined to do this, but accepted the concept and suggested that planning authorities should incorporate it into their new 'structure plans' under the 1968 Town and Country Planning Act. This proposal, and the 'heritage coast' concept, have met with widespread and enthusiastic acceptance; a number of counties are incorporating heritage coasts into the plans, and this should eventually give them a measure of protection not far short of that which the commission originally proposed. Moreover, it has used its experimental powers under the Countryside Act to finance the appointment of special heritage coast staff in three counties – Suffolk, Dorset and Glamorgan – and others are likely to follow. This move, which may be seen as analogous to the

The Nigg Bay oil rig construction site as seen from the Black Isle, above Cromarty town

D.O.E.'s payment of salaries of conservation officers in historic towns and districts, is extremely valuable. It means that there are expert, committed officers whose full-time job it is to conserve and enhance these areas. Unlike hard-pressed planning staff, they should have the time and the grass-roots knowledge of their areas to move over to creative planning, conservation and recreational management rather than simply reacting negatively to what has already begun. Moreover, the National Trust's Operation Neptune has now boosted the length of coastline which the Trust protects by ownership or covenant, from 179 miles in 1964 to 355 miles a decade later.

The picture is therefore a mixed one. On the one hand, recreational pressures on the coastline have probably never been greater; and industry increasingly demands waterside locations with deep-water berths for tankers and ore-carriers and cooling water for power stations and industrial processes. On the other hand, there are signs that the machinery for

controlling development is changing gear from one of belated,
inadequate and largely negative control to something more
creative and more sympathetic to the true spirit rather than the
letter of conservation. Certainly when the British coastline is
compared with many Mediterranean coasts, where commercial
or industrial development has spread with little or no restriction,
we have much to be thankful for.

1. Announcing plans to nationalize sites needed for North Sea oil opera-
tions, the Labour government gave two not altogether reconcilable
reasons for this course: prevention of acquisition delays, and prevention
of environmental damage.

2. At a conference on second homes called by the Town and Country
Planning Association in Birmingham in May 1974, Mr Daffydd Williams,
general secretary of Plaid Cymru, gave instances of areas in Wales where
the incidence of second homes was then already unacceptably high. They
accounted for 10 per cent of all dwellings in Anglesey, 15 per cent in the
Cemaes district of Pembrokeshire, and 20 per cent in the Lleyn peninsula.
In one village, Abersoch, 139 out of 248 homes were second ones; in
another, Rhyd, Merionethshire, every single one of the 40–50 dwellings
were now, according to Plaid, occupied only as second homes or holiday
accommodation.

1 THE HIGHWAYMEN

OF all the types of development that adversely affect both townscape and landscape in Britain, arguably the most destructive in the past two decades has been the building of roads. In the 1960s, the highwaymen really got into their stride with the motorway network, and only rarely could the entrenched rural conservationists do more than slightly deflect them from their purpose. It was perhaps only when the more expensive and destructive urban motorways threatened political repercussions in the marginal parliamentary seats of London and other big cities that their impetus was curbed, and a new enforced sensitivity both to public participation and environmental and aesthetic considerations began to prevail.

The trouble with road building, as compared with most other forms of development, is that it is linear. Once he begins a road, the road planner and engineer generally expects to be able to continue it. A new road funnelling into an old and inadequate one automatically creates pressure for fresh 'improvement'. A motorway built forty miles to the middle of nowhere demands to be extended and though, in theory, the decision may be subject to public consultation and inquiry, there is seldom any real possibility of doing more than deflecting the route or whittling down the width. Only once in a blue moon does the kind of opposition that built up to Toronto's Spadina Expressway succeed in stopping the highwaymen in mid-stride.

That was in part the dilemma of the very influential and articulate lobby who fought an extension of the M3 motorway from Popham in Hampshire. It was planned to run to the east of the cathedral city of Winchester, slicing the edge of the ancient water meadows that run up to the cathedral and college, then hurtling across country to join up with the semi-motorway Chandler's Ford bypass. These two stretches of modern, high-quality highway were there. In between came some indifferent, single carriageway road and the 1930s Winchester bypass, four-lane dual carriageway but by modern standards, with very tight curves and, in recent years, overloaded and with a bad accident record.

So at the public inquiry in 1971 argument turned on whether the road construction unit's 'preferred' route, running first one side and then the other of the old bypass, should stand, or whether some alternative to east or west through open country should be substituted. All of them were damaging in their various ways. For this reason, the conservationists were split. College and town opposed the preferred route and argued for one or other of two westerly rural routes. The Hampshire branch of C.P.R.E. (like the county planning committee) plumped reluctantly and with reservations for the preferred route. The Minister and his inspector gave judgement early in 1973 in its favour.

Loud and vehement were the protests. Peers made angry speeches in the House of Lords, well-known Wykehamists wrote long and eloquent letters to *The Times*, and the powerful Winchester M3 Action Group produced posters of a monstrous M3 skeleton towering over vulnerable medieval cloisters. The centuries' old tranquillity of the water meadows would be destroyed, the access of school and town to the beauty spot of St Catherine's Hill disrupted, they protested. The Editor of *The Times* was impressed. 'Go and have a look,' he said, 'Listen to the arguments on both sides.' I spent two days attempting to do so, and sadly came to the conclusion that all the routes were bad ones.[1] Both western routes cut through fine, unspoiled Hampshire countryside, with long views, wide hilltops, mature woods, little habitation and a sense of spaciousness that is now rare in populous and heavily trafficked southern England. The eastern route cut into even more attractive countryside, was considerably longer, and by far the most expensive. The preferred route, which (not by accident) was the cheapest, threw six lanes of traffic across the peaceful Upper Itchen Valley; scraped along the eastern edge of the city, creating severe noise problems to some tall blocks of council flats and nearby residential roads; and then ran past and through those water meadows, half a mile from the cathedral and college, to pass within 500 yards of the medieval settlement of St Cross. 'It will turn the cathedral and college precinct into a noise slum,' said the route's opponents. 'The old bypass of the thirties is already an intrusion,' said the road engineers. 'With the earth mounding and tree planting we propose, the new road, though wider, will be less of an intrusion both in terms of noise and visual disturbance.'

One remains sceptical. What is clear, however, is that the effects of these twelve miles of M3 now being built by the D.O.E.'s regional construction unit do not cease when the blue signs say 'End of motorway'. A severer impact by far, to my mind, comes with the new roads the city itself planned (and the new county is presumably building) to link with Winchester's two M3 interchanges. They do run 'through' the city; they will sever one neighbourhood from another, running through inner areas which, though not (except for a few buildings) medieval, continue the scale and texture of the medieval city. They will bring constant traffic noise and movement to the edge of the now partially pedestrianized historic centre. And here again the

Left: The present
Winchester by-pass
with St Cross church
in the background.
The new M.3 will run
across the intervening
meadows. Above:
Houses to be
demolished to
accommodate link
roads from the
motorway to the city
centre

highwaymen's awful logic is apparent. If the mistaken decision
of the 1930s to align the original bypass on the cathedral side
of the city made an M3 routing on that side almost unstoppable
in 1973, so too a decision of the 1950s to place the new Hampshire County Council headquarters in the centre of the city and
not outside, produced an ever-increasing traffic movement in
the town that demanded an improved 'distributor' system
there. With hindsight, the logic is not quite unshakeable. On
the local roads at least, Winchester could have had its Spadina.
But its citizens, and especially the articulate middle-class ones,
do lean heavily on the use of their motor-cars. As one resident
in the Kingsgate Street area near the college tartly remarked the
morning after a packed protest meeting nearby, they registered
unanimous opposition to the road and the damage that the
traffic it would carry threatened to an historic setting; then the
meeting broke up to a tumultuous applause and a sustained
banging of car doors and revving of car engines.

Glasgow, next to Birmingham the British city most banged
about by the highwaymen, is quite another case. It has a much
lower than average car ownership, yet the city fathers have
staked all on providing virtually unrestricted access for the
motor vehicle to the very edge of a tightly confined central
area. To date, the eastern side of their motorway box has been
built, bridging the Clyde spectacularly and not unattractively;
and a northern side, which has cleared a swathe through the

inner city and left communities severed and desolate waste lands where there were grim but sociable tenements. But it is the proposed east side of the box that really threatens the worst damage. Most people in the south probably think of Glasgow as a large industrial and commercial city, and in no sense an historic town. Yet it is historic. It was one of Britain's first cathedral cities and one of the earliest university cities. Defoe called it 'the beautifulest little city in Europe'. Though that description is scarcely now applicable, Glasgow has many architectural glories. It had also many slums, and in its determination to get rid of those the city fathers have often fallen into the trap of knocking down attractive buildings (or permitting them to be knocked down) simply because they were old.

The road programme proposed in 1965 was immense. It took

the lion's share of a £485m transportation plan for Greater Glasgow: public transport's share was to be only £65m. With a target date of 1990, the plan envisaged the building of 285 miles of motorway in the Glasgow region. The prime element of its public transport proposals was the electrification of eighty-three more miles of railway. The New Glasgow Society, formed as a reaction to large-scale compulsory purchase in the inner areas, argued that the plan was grotesquely out of balance. Fine buildings and long-established communities were being destroyed because of the city's enthusiasm for pulling down buildings just because they were old and for building roads which most Glaswegians were unlikely to make use of.

The balance of opinion has changed. Schemes like the city complex of roads and motorways at Charing Cross on the east side of the motorway box, which tore a great empty swathe in the fabric of the city and attempted to force people on foot over long and exposed ramped bridges if they needed to follow the old patterns of movement on foot, did much to change Glasgow people's attitudes. So did the attitude of some leading city councillors towards fine buildings in the city's Victorian merchant quarter, described by Pevsner on a visit as among the world's great nineteenth-century cities.[2] Though the city might quote a Secretary of State for Scotland as saying of the east and west flanks of the box 'It is a bold and imaginative part of an integrated development which aims at providing an old but re-juvenating city with a modern system of road communications and a forward looking pattern of redevelopment at the same time,' Scottish secretaries more than once felt obliged to cut the city engineer's highway plans down to size. In its first battle, the new Glasgow Society persuaded the reporter* at a public inquiry on the 'improvement' of the Great Western Road that a less damaging widening catering for 30,000 vehicles a day instead of the proposed 40,000 was enough. The road's boulevard quality was spared and its frontages saved from the most acute effects of proximity to traffic.

But the east flank of the box, despite strong arguments that it is not needed, cannot be afforded, or could give the edge of the central city a wider berth. is still firmly in the city council's plans. People began to realize in 1972 just what it threatened: six lanes of motorway, often on stilts, plus slip roads, ploughing along the line or too close to the line of Glasgow's ancient High Street (once the centre but now on the eastern edge of the centre of the town). Of the buildings it affected just a few were the seventeenth-century Tollbooth Steeple (motorway line 20–30ft away); a fine range of College Residences by the Adam Brothers

* The Scottish equivalent of inspector

(since demolished by the corporation), and the Martyrs' Public School (one of the few remaining buildings by Glasgow's great Victorian architect, Charles Rennie Mackintosh), whose proposed demolition drew a rare protest from the Royal Institute of British Architects.[3] Two churches, St Andrew's Parish church and the fine mid-eighteenth-century St Andrew's by the Green, would both have their setting wrecked by the road. By February 1974, however, the corporation abandoned the original line, bending the road more to the east clear of the Tollbooth at Glasgow Cross, though not far enough away to satisfy the anti-motorway lobby that it would be acceptable environmentally. The Highways Committee convener, Mr Tom Fulton, claimed 'Our officials and consultants appear to have reconciled to the maximum possible extent the criticism of the so-called original line. We have avoided the historic core of the city.'[4] Not, however, before demolishing those College Residences, the last Adam building in the illustrious brothers' native city. The argument about the acceptability of the new route may however well be academic. Even in Glasgow the official tide is turning against roads and in favour of more public transport. The new public transport authority has proposed to spend £26·5m on a Clyde Rail network of improved, electrified train services; their modernization of parts of Glasgow's small but useful underground is also in hand. While in mid-1974 funds for public transport were scarce, for new urban road schemes they looked as though they were going to be virtually non-existent. Convener Fulton conceded that the east flank could scarcely be started for another five or six years and that the decision whether or not to go ahead would lie not with Glasgow Corporation but with the new Strathclyde regional council which was due to take over responsibility for transport in April 1975. It will probably never be built.

In Edinburgh, the highwaymen were stopped in their tracks very much earlier. Scotland's capital is a very middle-class city with influential lawyers, civil servants and other professionals reinforcing the amenity lobby. Unlike Glasgow, where an entrenched Labour majority on the council is so secure that it can afford to be unresponsive to minority protests, Edinburgh has in postwar years mostly had a fine party balance on the city council: the old ruling group, the Progressives, were under fire not only from Labour but also from a minority Conservative group with strongly conservationist, anti-roads views.

Edinburgh too was to have its motorway box, but popular opposition, professional argument, and adroit political manoeuvring dismembered it bit by bit and eventually killed it.

The north flank would have inflicted fatal wounds on the city's Georgian 'New Town'. The west flank similarly so. The south flank would have ploughed through the Meadows on the south side of the town ruining one of the city's most attractive and well-appreciated open spaces. The east flank (which survived longest) would have thrust itself brutally across the Royal Mile of the old city, with slip roads running close to Holyrood Palace and Calton Hill, like a huge vacuum cleaner poised to draw traffic into the city, though scarcely (as the then engineer claimed) to free it of congestion.

A long and valiant battle against what many people considered the then city Engineer's delusions of grandeur was fought by Colin Buchanan & Partners as consultants to the corporation. The Buchanan team's proposals in October 1972 to scale down even the east flank drastically and build up public transport with priority busways met bitter opposition in the city engineer's department but, such was the change in public and political opinion in the city, within seven months had been thrown over as too road-oriented. The latest irony came in June 1974 when the city engaged new consultants to look into a light-rail-based public transport system instead. The Buchanan team had abandoned this attractive possibility because British Rail were reluctant to make available one vital pair of tracks for its use. Now things have changed. The new consultants were reported to be getting the enthusiastic co-operation of British Rail.

Sometimes a road destructive of fine landscape is pushed through against weighty opposition by political pressure for development. Such was the case of the A66 through the Lake District, now being 'improved' on such a scale as to change its nature. The main pressure for a new road came from the economically depressed west Cumberland towns which have long suffered from poor links with the main north-south route now represented by the M6. Indeed, some sort of a government promise of such a road was one of the factors that induced Lord Stokes to site a Leyland factory at Workington.

At the public inquiry into this long delayed project, argument turned not on the need for a new road, which is undoubted, but the route to be followed. (As we have seen, it is extremely difficult to argue at an inquiry that a new road along a given route is not needed at all.) The preferred solution, now approved by the Minister and being built, follows the line of the present A66 from the M6 interchange near Penrith with new sections of route near Troutbeck and Scale. Their effect will be to substitute for a single carriageway road which follows contours and curves and has settled into the landscape, a much broader straighter road, which defies these contours. Familiar long views from Keswick over Bassenthwaite Lake will be drastically affected by a new four-mile bypass to the north of Keswick, and the road is then to run along the western shore of the Lake, with new embankments extending into the water. For the route it was argued that in many of these places a road or an old railway track already exists. The Friends of the Lake District, who opposed the scheme, reply that there is a great deal of difference between these established lines, which curve and follow the contours, and a new road, even if not dual carriageway, designed to higher engineering standards and therefore less able to thread over and round and down in tune with the shape of the ground.

The Friends, and the Countryside Commission, proposed an alternative route running through attractive countryside to the north – outside the National Park boundary – largely on existing A and B class roads. The Minister allowed it to be investigated jointly by D.O.E. and Countryside Commission officials and it was eventually put to the inquiry as an alternative to the official route. The reasons given for sticking to the original line are, to many people, not at all convincing. The alternative route passes through very attractive countryside, but it is undulating and well wooded and a road of this scale would largely have disappeared into it. The pleasant little village of Sebergham (pronounced 'See-bur-um') would have needed protection by means of a generous bypass, but otherwise in environmental terms it seemed to have few snags. It would certainly have avoided scarring the grandeur of those long views near Troutbeck which depend on a contrast of scale between the broad valley and high fells and the smallness of natural and manmade detail – such as trees, walls, farmsteads, and the existing road.

A clearer distinction ought also to have been drawn between the two types of traffic demand for the road. One is holiday traffic seeking to reach Keswick and points beyond, mostly consisting of private cars which (a) do not cause so much congestion on the narrow road and (b) as 'optional' traffic might arguably have been expected to tolerate some congestion at peak summer weekends. The other is the relatively small but increasing and important flows of heavy commercial vehicles, such as tankers from chemical and detergent works at Whitehaven, which could be expected to follow the rather longer route to the north if it gave a time saving, and anyway might reasonably have been obliged to use that route by an 'Except for access' weight limit on the A66.

Evening light on planned A66 two-level interchange site, as seen from Latriff looking over the upper Naddle Valley to Helvellyn. The present A66 runs in front of Briery cottages (on extreme left) across the picture. The interchange with its embankments, cuttings, bridge and convolutions will cover the whole of the foreground field and demolish the cottages. Work is now in progress on this site. The cottages have been demolished

The Friends of the Lake District summed up the objection to the A66 route under five heads:

(1) A major industrial highway should not be brought through Britain's premier national park.

(2) The vast engineering works involved are completely out of keeping with the small, intimate scale of the Lake District.

(3) The route round Keswick, with its viaduct and motorway interchange (a land-consuming, free-flow, multi-level structure) will alter the whole character of this fine unspoiled background of the town.

(4) Fast dual carriageways along the western shores of Bassenthwaite will destroy its natural setting.

(5) There is a good valid alternative route for industrial traffic to West Cumberland.[5]

Below: Work on the Keswick bypass section of the A66, July 1974. Far left: The A66 has recently altered at Naddle Bank. New road now planned to replace it would cross middle distance. Skiddaw and Lonsdale Fell in background. Left: A66 at Threlkfield bypass: standard carriageway, standard verges, concrete kerbs and a failure to follow the curve of the contour

Their objections failed to move the Minister or, indeed, to convince some local people. A main reason, I think, must be failure of imagination. Few people can visualize the size and nature of new civil engineering works or their impact on landscape before they happen. Even fewer can appreciate in advance the effect, not just of the structures, but of the constantly moving streams of traffic on them. They tend to take existing tranquillity for granted – until it has gone.

Much the same argument about whether to route new roads through or round National Parks has been going on in the Peak District, where the park planning board has strenuously argued that motorways to east, west, north and south of the park might be acceptable; motorways through it were not. 'Minor' road improvements in the park have been bad enough, says the board's director, Theo Burrell. A little widening here and straightening there may ease congestion and improve a road's physical capacity, but in the sensitive landscape of a national park it may both cause visual damage and lead to the area's 'environmental capacity' being exceeded.

Lorry traffic at
Westgate, Warwick

Tourist 'blunderbuses' manoeuvring in Oxford High Street

One argument sometimes used to bolster the case for roads like the second Sheffield-Manchester motorway which now threatens the northern Peak District is that selfish conservationists should not try to deny the urban masses car-borne access to their countryside heritage. 'What is the use of a national park if you cannot get to it easily?' they ask. This is a fallacious argument. People who want to enjoy national park scenery do not need to drive at seventy miles an hour into the heart of it in order to do so. And if road building destroys or depreciates the thing they came to see, it is a poor service to them to build it there. Of course, it is pleasant to drive from Sheffield to Manchester through striking scenery (as you may on the existing M62 across the Pennines). But if that pleasure conflicts with the amenity of people actually using the countryside, it is not to be reckoned of very high priority. A combination of shortage of money for new roads, and the realization that car use in popular areas of countryside may have to be curtailed and people offered alternative means of reaching them, may yet combine to save the Peak District from this threat.

Roads do not, however, have to be motorways or be continuous routes to damage the landscape. The need for a bypass to Petworth is long standing and undisputed. The narrow streets and sharp bends of this little Sussex town were never meant for today's heavy traffic, let alone for the heavy lorries which daily lumber over pavements and almost weekly knock chunks off walls and corners of buildings. Five busy A roads meet there, and the town groans under the weight of them.

But where to put the bypass? West Sussex county council found itself in a quandary. To the west of the town lies Petworth House, its tall stone boundary walls hemming the town in tightly; its park, landscaped by Capability Brown and with a rare herd of 400 deer, stretching away to the west and northwest, all owned by the National Trust. To the east of the town lie the sloping meadows on either side of Shimmings Brook, an attractive valley with walks and footpaths. Townspeople have traditionally used this for recreation rather than Petworth Park, to which access is restricted, though less so now than in the past.

A route through the park would be shortest, cheapest and affect fewest houses, argued the county council, choosing that answer in 1951 and again in 1965. The National Trust opposed it and would be ready to invoke their special right to a parliamentary hearing. The townspeople intensely dislike the Shimmings Brook route and their dislike was intensified by memories of long-standing bad relations between town and the Egremont family, once owners of, and now the National Trust's tenants at, the house. So the trust called in Buchanan & Partners who produced a route further to the east, avoiding most of the valley, but adversely affecting some houses at Byworth, a village to the east. This route was calculated to cost between £500,000 and £1m more than the park route at 1973 prices.

The county council, wanting to do the right thing in terms of public participation, in September 1973 put on an exhibition of the alternative, cheaper, routes. Its road engineer claimed that a road through the park could be contoured and landscaped 'so that it could hardly be seen from Petworth House, 700 yards away'. The National Trust and Buchanan both believed the contrary: that the tranquillity of the park and the quality of the landscape itself – some of the finest eighteenth-century park landscape in Britain – would be seriously damaged. Walking over the two routes at that time, I could not but be acutely aware of the dilemma. How do you weigh against each other fine landscape and people's domestic peace and quiet? Yet man-made landscape of that quality is a work of art. Driving a road through it´would have been to destroy a unique masterpiece which Turner, visiting Petworth, admired and celebrated in oils. However well 'landscaped', a road through the park, I concluded, would be tantamount to the county's road engineers going armed with knives to the National Gallery and scoring deep gashes across a Turner landscape.[6] Was there not some other solution? Later signs have been encouraging. The county surveyor offered a new solution – basically, the park route but with the road cut more deeply into the ground and covered in the most sensitive places. This cut-and-cover solution, which would possibly go most of the way to deadening noise and might well remove all visual intrusion, is now the subject of a full-scale design study, and both the D.O.E. and the National Trust have supported the study and promised to look at the results sympathetically. They are committed to no more than that, but this is one highwaymen's hold-up that could have a happy ending.

Petworth Park. The proposed bypass would have crossed the middle ground in a shallow cutting. Inset: The same scene as painted by Turner

1. *The Times*, 7 March 1973; see also *The Architects' Journal*, 26 September 1973
2. Pevsner, Nikolaus, *The Buildings of England: London 1*, Penguin, revised 1972
3. Letter from the Secretary of the R.I.B.A. to the Town Clerk of Glasgow, reported in *The Times*, 5 October 1974
4. *Glasgow Herald*, 26 February 1974
5. *The Lake District Threatened*, Friends of the Lake District, 1972
6. *The Times*, 6 September 1973

ALBERT DOCK. LIVERPO
STUDIES FOR CONVERSION TO LIVERPO
DESIGNED BY: BUILDING DESIGN PART
DRAWN BY: ALAN MITCHELL

OLYTECHNIC
P, ARCHITECTS

12 TURN OF THE TIDE

I N chronicling some of the drastic and disastrous changes that have occurred on the face of Britain during the postwar decades, and especially the sixties and seventies, I have given some signs of changes for the better. To be sure the air sometimes seemed full, in the months in which I researched and wrote this book, of environmental voices prophesying doom. But this paradoxically may have been itself a hopeful sign. The so-called energy crisis, along with all manner of shortages of, and high prices for, basic materials have made a significant impact during 1974. The change to an integrated system of transport planning with block grants to cover both roads and public transport should mean, especially in the conurbations, that the lion's share will now go, not in a vain attempt to satisfy the voracious demands of the private motor-car by building ever more expensive and destructive roads, but on mass public transport, whose impact (even when its artefacts are new ones) is generally much less damaging to the environment than roads and motor traffic. Moreover, determined and resourceful political battling by groups such as Barbara Maude's Transport Reform Group has produced changes in the manner of examining and deciding major road lines which put local communities in a very much better position to influence these decisions. They can now confront the inspector conducting such an inquiry with evidence that a road is not needed on the scale proposed or even that it is not needed at all. Whether an inspector will ever feel able to advise the Minister to this effect, saying boldly that national roads policy is wrong, is a different matter. But the change is an advance which seemed unlikely only two or three years ago, and it does place one more slight curb on a particularly damaging agent of change.

Similarly, in our towns and cities the tide is turning – sometimes too late, when the damage has been done; not always so. By the middle of 1974 the steam had gone out of large-scale office development. This was mostly the result of economic recession and economies in public expenditure. But an encouraging number of organizations and individuals were converting old buildings when previously they would have been demolished and replaced, or going in for small-scale sympathetic infill rather than larger-scale clear-and-rebuild development. The approach of European Architectural Heritage Year was a factor; but so too were the warning lights that had started flashing in the minds of architects and planners and their clients and masters during the curious period in the winter of 1973/74 when petrol was hard to come by and a combination of world shortage and the three-day-week had made some aspects of

construction design previously taken for granted seem at least questionable. Altogether there was a sense that these professions had overreached themselves, been over-ambitious in their long-term planning and prodigal in their use of all manner of resources.

This current of opinion was summed up vividly at two annual conferences in the summer of 1974 – the Royal Town Planning Institute in London in June, and the Royal Institute of British Architects at Durham in July. The R.T.P.I.'s president, architect planner Graham Ashworth, called for 'a re-think in every planning office' with the profession re-examining 'all their precepts, to see where they are based on unlimited availability of resources'.[1] They should, he urged them, begin to recast their plans to 'maximize renewable resources, including the human resource.' At the R.I.B.A. conference, another architect planner, Walter Bor (international town planning consultant and, significantly, former city planning officer of Liverpool),[2] was explicit and outspoken in his admission of the profession's past mistakes. Misled by 'over-optimistic assumptions about available resources in terms of money, materials and labour', they had over-concentrated their efforts on 'too many costly and over-ambitious schemes for city centre rebuilding, often aggravating congestion and entailing poorly

179

designed megastructures and high buildings; on too many motorways badly integrated with the urban environment; and on too much residential redevelopment in the course of which we have disrupted cohesive communities'.[3]

Both conferences seemed explicitly or tacitly to endorse tougher restraint on the private motor-car, because it was realized that even modest urban motorway systems do intolerable damage to urban fabric, and the more ambitious ones destroy the city without even coming near to satisfying an expanding demand for road space. This policy is seen at potentially its toughest in Nottingham, where a system of 'zones and collars' will constrict the peak hour flow of private cars into the city in proportion as congestion builds up in the centre and on its approaches.[4] But in Nottingham, as in a score of other towns, the obverse of this restraint is being demonstrated. As cars are restrained, the pedestrian is being liberated. In the centre of Leeds, shopping and walking conditions have been transformed by the paving over of more than three-quarters of a mile of existing streets. Vehicles are not banned altogether, simply relegated to second-class status. The pedestrian is king.[5] And as he walks easy in his kingdom, he looks at the cleaned and repainted buildings, and the trees and seats and fountains that have replaced traffic congestion, and he sees that the city is now a good place to linger in, not somewhere he must escape from. In Stevenage new town, it was found cheaper to subsidize a really good bus service than to build expensive and visually destructive flyovers and underpasses. On its first experimental route, the Superbus runs every five minutes to within five minutes of almost every front door in the neighbourhood it serves. It is, they say, always there or just round the corner. It has trebled the number of passenger rides from that neighbourhood in its first three years, and the system is being extended.[6] On Tyneside and in Sheffield they are planning to bring back something very like the tram.

In the field of historic buildings, a far more generous listing policy is being adopted to give statutory protection to buildings which previously would not have been considered to merit it. More important, imaginative and economic uses are being found for them. Rum warehouses on Thameside at Deptford have been kept to lend eighteenth-century grace and contrast to a public housing project – but not just kept, converted. The result is sixty-five fine flats whose cost was not much more than two-thirds of the cost of comparable new homes had they been built there.[7] In Liverpool the city council abandoned plans to rehouse its polytechnic in tower blocks surrounded by motorways and is instead housing them in the 130-year-old warehouse buildings of Albert Dock, Grade I listed buildings for which conservationists had almost despaired of finding a viable use. The conversion will provide better accommodation more quickly, more cheaply and with more potential for expansion than the original scheme would have done.[8] Far from being unsuitable, these fine Victorian buildings have all the qualities that a past president of the R.I.B.A., Alex Gordon, sought to promote in his Long Life/Loose Fit/Low Energy study. They are admirably robust, easily adaptable and suffer minimum heat loss and solar gain. They are also, in planning terms, in the right part of the city and, preserved by a lively new use, will continue as an adornment to the waterside as well as an integrating force socially rather than a divisive one.

Liverpool's Albert
Dock, now to be
restored
Inset: The interior of
the long 'C' block

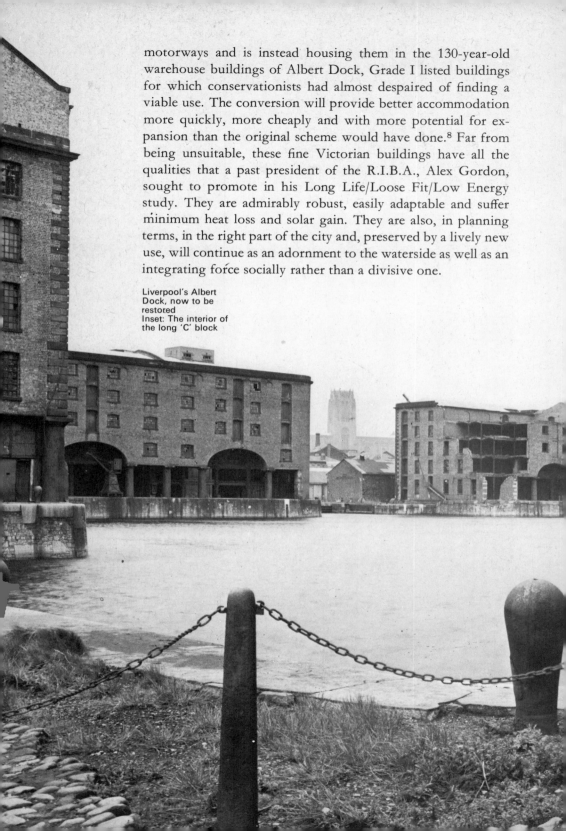

Opposite above: Early 19th-century brick houses at Holywell, Clwyd, restored and converted into old peoples' sheltered housing (architects: Lingard & Associates)

Opposite below: Rum warehouses at Pepys Estate, Deptford, converted into flats by the G.L.C.

Below left: Maltings at Beccles, now houses, pub and restaurant (architects: Feilden & Mawson)

Left: Flight of 23 locks on Kennet and Avon Canal at Devizes, Wilts — still to be restored

Below: Chancellor's courtyard, Leeds University (architects: Chamberlin, Powell & Bon)

Derelict land
reclamation at
Stoke-on-Trent. Top
left: Sneyd tip before
reclamation and (top

right) after
reclamation. Bottom
left: Central Forest
Park before
reclamation and

(bottom right) after
reclamation (Land
Use Consultants with
Stoke-on-Trent parks
department)

In the past, some conservationists feared that if the countryside were saved from industrial development and destruction of its landscape, it would be destroyed by the recreational explosion. There are now hopeful signs that we are learning to guide and civilize that explosion. Five years ago that environmental Cinderella, the canal system, seemed, despite the hard work and enthusiasm of many devotees, to be falling apart. What road and housing development spared, lack of money for maintenance threatened. Money is still lacking, but the climate of official opinion has been transformed. Local authorities now regard canals not as something to be filled in but to be opened

up. And routes long since lost, like the Montgomery Arm of the Shropshire Union and the Wey and Arun from the Thames to the sea, are now being actively and confidently restored. Even projects for widening of commercial canals to take the weight off crowded urban roads, for the first time look a realistic proposition.

Another area in which dramatic improvements have been achieved is land reclamation. The outstanding case here, to my mind, is Stoke-on-Trent. Twenty years ago, its 'Six Towns' were interspersed by the accumulated rubbish of more than two centuries of intensive, heedless industrial activity. Grim, huge pit heaps towered above the little terraces; great marl-holes opened at your feet big enough to swallow a hundred houses; and everywhere ran derelict railway lines which the Beeching Axe had closed but done nothing to reinstate. Now two decades of steady effort by the city and their advisers Land Use Consultants already show what miracles a new tradition of large-scale landscape architecture can work. They are armed with mechanical aids Repton and Capability Brown never had; but they mould contours and plant trees not for a rich client and his privileged friends, but for the man from Town Road out with the dog, the kids from Bank Top kicking a ball or riding a bike. For them the Six Towns are being transformed. Recontoured pit heaps become green hills with the beginnings of a wood on them; a marl pit becomes (when almost but not quite filled in with colliery spoil) a lake for paddling in; and the black scars of abandoned railway lines become planted and landscaped 'Greenways', safe and pleasant places to walk or ride a bike, linking the open spaces together.

These are some of the hopeful signs. They are developments which need and merit encouragement. They should not blind us to the continuing threats and dangers. Farewells are not always sad nor is all change destructive. But too many good-byes to familiar bits of Britain in the last two decades have been tragic and could have been averted. The turning tide needs plenty of help from individual citizens to keep it running in the right direction.

1. *The Times*, 14 June 1974
2. *The Times*, 22 July 1974
3. *The Architects' Journal*, 10 July 1974
4. *The Architects' Journal*, 10 July 1974
5. *Illustrated London News,* September 1974, p. 71; *Outlook* (Bristol & West Building Society), summer 1973
6. *New Society*, 28 March 1974
7. *The Times*, 11 July 1974; *Country Life*, 11 July 1974
8. For a full account see *Illustrated London News*, August 1974

Conservation can aid the housing effort

Conservation is one of those Humpty-Dumpty words whose meaning varies with the intentions of the user. 'When *I* use a word,' said Humpty-Dumpty in Lewis Carroll's *Through the Looking-Glass*, 'it means just what I choose it to mean – neither more or less.' There are plenty of Humpty-Dumpties in the current environmental battle of words, and many confusingly multi-purpose words – not least *environment* itself, which means a multitude of different things to different people. Sometimes, moreover, they are unreasonably put out on discovering that you have not immediately perceived their particular meaning. It may be helpful, therefore, to start with a few definitions.

The word *conservation* can mean husbanding the world's natural resources, maintaining ecological balance among living things and preventing pollution which threatens 'ecocatastrophe'; it can mean saving wild stretches of open country from invasion by mining companies, building development or even tourism; it can mean protecting rare flora and fauna from such invasions; or it can mean (in the sense that the Conservation Society primarily uses it) keeping down human population so as to limit the strains which people in their sheer numbers impose on the world's finite resources.

But it can also mean – and this is the kind of conservation I want to talk about here – the appreciation of and practical caring for the appearance, scale, atmosphere and character of built-up places, whether they are historic cities like York or Bath, small market towns, suburbs or bits of cities, villages, odd rows of cottages, or individual buildings.

Not preservation

Even in this urban sense, however, the word *conservation* is – because of its very popularity – in danger of being misunderstood and devalued. To start with, it is not the same thing as what used to be called *preservation*. One can think of at least four important differences. First, preservation of old buildings is a defensive, negative stance: a reaction to the threat of demolition or decay. Conservation ought to be an attacking stance: the positive seeking out of new uses for old buildings or adaptation of old uses to make them viable.

Second, preservation has been largely a matter of individual buildings, generally those of special value architecturally or of special historical interest. These are the two tests applied in the Department of the Environment's statutory listings, which make demolition and alteration subject to official control. Conservation is concerned not so much with individual buildings as with 'places' – townscapes, groups of buildings and their surroundings, and what goes on in them.

Which brings us to difference No. 3. Preservation has traditionally largely been a matter of buildings regarded visually: fine pieces of architecture. Conservation goes further than that. It is not enough nowadays to save a building's skin, preserving it as an empty adornment to the urban scene. Museum pieces are not the conservationist answer. Instead we look for practical, reasonably economic uses; we look at the people who will use them; and whether the buildings and their surroundings are 'good environment'. We look at communities, how they function; and at what people like about the places where they live and what they find depressing or frustrating.

A fourth difference follows from this, which applies even to people's visual appreciation of buildings and their surroundings. Preservation rests on expert judgement of the architectural beauty or importance of a building. It is, say the Ministry investigators, one of the best Queen Anne houses in London, or important for its place in the development of architectural style.

Familiar faces

Conservation can be at once more subjective and more relative in its judgements. It can say: 'In itself this building isn't much, but it's the best this particular locality has, and the loss would be more serious here than in other places where Ministry-listed buildings are two a penny.' Or it can say: 'This building is nothing architecturally, but it is an important landmark – a familiar point of reference in a neighbourhood where everything else has changed or is changing. It ought to be kept as people's one link with the past.' This is true, in town and country, of many a spire of a redundant Victorian church which crowns a vista or makes a landscape. Such stable points in a changing urban scene are, psychologically, part of people's sense of identity – landmarks they need to hang on to, like friendly neighbours or familiar faces. We uproot them at our peril.

A fifth and most crucial difference is that conserving the character of an area does not mean a blanket 'No' to redevelopment. It means keeping what is best while ensuring that replacement is in harmony with its surroundings. New buildings infilling the street scene need not – and usually should not – ape their neighbours; but, in scale, colour, texture of materials and such important visual elements as vertical or horizontal emphasis, they should be in harmony – should be sympathetic, good-mannered new neighbours.

Reprinted by kind permission of the Bristol & West Building Society from *Outlook,* their magazine on conservation and housing topics.

INDEX

ACKNOWLEDGEMENTS

Tony Aldous 43, 46–47, 48–49; Peter Ambrose, 142; Architects' Journal/Dan Cruikshank 88–89, 162, 163; Bailey 21; Peter Baker Library 133; Geoffrey Berry 169, 170, 171; Birmingham, City Engineers' Dept 28, 31, 33; Lewis Braithwaite 32; Brecht Einzig Ltd 96; Bristol and West 35; BP 150–151; British Tourist Authority 62, 126; Patrick Brown 45; Building Design Partnership 176–177, 182–183; Camera Press/Colin Davey 8, 18–19, 19, 26–27, 84–85; Hamish Campbell 156–157; Capital and Counties 36; J. Allan Cash 11, 91, 123; F. J. Cooper 17; K. F. Evans 56, 57; Fielden and Mawson, architects 185; Forestry Commission 125, 129; Grant's Studio 147; GLC Photo Library 73, 79, 92–93, 101, 104, 114, 184; Handfords 93, 108–109; Christopher Hanson 144–145, 146; A. F. Kersting 68, 69; Keystone 98–99, 102, 158–159; Sam Lambert 113; Henry Law 116–117, 117; Legal and General 49; Dennis Lennon and Partners 86–87; London Borough of Islington 113; London Borough of Lewisham 114; Charles McKean 164; John McKean 2–3, 186–187; John Maltby 185; Manchester Guardian 14–15; Jerry Mason 66–67; Geoffrey Mayor 172–173; National Trust/Jeremy Whitaker 175; Newcastle-City Engineers' Dept 39, 41; Newcastle-University 40; Northampton Chronicle and Echo 50–51, 54–55, 57; Peak Park Planning Board 136–137, 149; Phoebus 20, 74; Popperfoto 68, 71; Derek Pratt 185; Henk Snoek 114; Steven Development Corporation 179, 18 Tamworth Castle Museum 59, Times 81; Topham Picture Library 118–119, 122, 122–123 Topix 48; Patrick Ward 93; Paul Watkins 64–65, 72–73, 7 74, 82–83, 95, 111; West–En Photography 130; Colin Westwoo 41; World Trade Centre 76

192